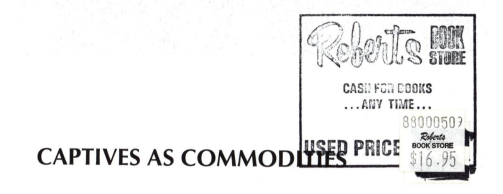

CAPTIVES AS COMMODITIES

D0207427

Connections: Key Themes in World History

CAPTIVES AS COMMODITIES

The Transatlantic Slave Trade

Lisa A. Lindsay
The University of North Carolina at Chapel Hill

Upper Saddle River, New Jersey 07458

Library of Congress Cataloging-in-Publication Data

Lindsay, Lisa A.
  The Atlantic slave trade / Lisa A. Lindsay.
    p. cm.
  Includes bibliographical references and index.
  ISBN 13: 978-0-13-194215-8 (alk. paper)
  ISBN 10: 0-13-194215-8
  1. Slave trade—Africa—History.   2. Slave-trade—Europe—History.
3. Slave trade—America—History.   I. Title.

HT1321.L56 2008
382'.44—dc22

2007030501

Executive Editor: Charles Cavaliere
Senior Editorial Assistant: Maureen Diana
Senior Marketing Manager: Kate Mitchell
Marketing Assistant: Jennifer Lang
Production Liaison: Joanne Riker
Creative Design Director: Jayne Conte
Cover Designer: Bruce Kenselaar
Cover Illustration/Photo:
Director Image Resource Center: Melinda Reo
Manager, Rights and Permissions:
  Zina Arabia

Image Permission Coordinator:
  Angelique Sharps
Manager, Visual Research: Beth Brenzel
Manager, Cover Visual Research &
  Permissions: Karen Sanatar
Photo Researcher: Rebecca Harris
Composition/Full-Service Project
  Management: Integra Software
  Services Pvt. Ltd.
Printer/Binder: RR Donnelley

Credits and acknowledgments borrowed from other sources and reproduced, with permission,
in this textbook appear on appropriate page within text.

Pearson Education Ltd.
Pearson Education Singapore, Pte. Ltd.
Pearson Education, Canada, Ltd.
Pearson Education—Japan

Pearson Education Australia PTY, Ltd.
Pearson Education North Asia Ltd
Pearson Educación de Mexico, S.A. de C.V.
Pearson Education Malaysia, Pte. Ltd.

10 9 8 7 6 5 4 3 2 1
ISBN 13: 978-0-13-194215-8
ISBN 10:   0-13-194215-8

ontents

Foreword

Connections: Key Themes in World History focuses on specific issues of world historical significance from antiquity to the present by employing a combination of explanatory narrative, primary sources, questions relating to those sources, a summary analysis ("Making Connections"), and further points to ponder, all of which combine to enable readers to discover some of the most important driving forces in world history.

The increasingly rapid pace and specialization of historical inquiry has created an ever-widening gap between professional publications and general surveys, especially surveys of world history. The purpose of *Connections* is to bridge that gap by placing the latest research and debates on selected topics of global historical significance, as well as some of the evidence upon which historians base their insights, into a form and context that is comprehensible to students and general readers alike.

Two pedagogical principles infuse this series. First, students master world history most easily if allowed to focus on specific themes and issues. Such themes, by their very specificity, as well as because of their general application, enable students to perceive and understand the overall patterns and meaning of our shared global past more clearly than is possible through reading, by itself, a massive world history textbook. Second, students learn best when asked to think critically about what they are studying. So far as the study of history is concerned, critical thinking necessarily involves analysis of primary sources.

To that end, we offer a series of brief, tightly focused books that embrace a radical simplicity and a provocative format. Each book goes to the heart of a key theme, phenomenon, or issue in world history—something that has connected humans across cultures, continents, and time spans. By actively engaging with this material, the reader comes to understand in a nuanced and meaningful manner how often distantly located human cultures have been connected to one another as key actors in the epic story of world history.

Alfred J. Andrea
Series Editor
Professor Emeritus of History
University of Vermont

Series Editor's Preface

A snowy St. Patrick's Day, March 17, 2007. Three days ago, Prime Minister Tony Blair delivered a public apology for Great Britain's role in the transatlantic slave trade. The date Prime Minister Blair chose is significant because it was the halfway point between two 200-year anniversaries.

On March 2, 1807, President Thomas Jefferson signed into law a bill prohibiting the importation of slaves into the United States, effective January 1, 1808. On the face of it, the measure was a major blow against the Atlantic slave trade, but appearances can be deceiving. The bill provided that slaves intercepted and seized under this law would be confiscated as contraband and disposed of by the relevant federal district court in accordance with the laws of the state in which they were seized. Hence, slaves seized in Southern states would be auctioned off as property and not freed. Moreover, those found guilty of importing slaves would be fined. The crime, in effect, was a misdemeanor, and given this light sanction, the transport of enslaved human cargo into the United States continued, although at a reduced level. U.S. ships were also not prohibited from carrying slaves to other countries and colonies in the Western Hemisphere where the slave trade was legal and flourishing, such as Brazil and Cuba. Despite the best attempts of abolitionists to inaugurate a peaceful process leading to the eventual eradication of African slavery in the United States, this law did not signal the proverbial beginning of the end. It would take four bitter years of Civil War, some 600,000 dead soldiers, and the Thirteenth Amendment to the Constitution of 1865 to achieve that end.

On March 25, 1807, King George III gave royal approval to An Act for the Abolition of the Slave Trade (also effective January 1, 1808) that had passed the House of Commons by a vote of 114 to 15 and the House of Lords by 41 to 20, in the latter, thanks in large part to the oratory of Lord Grenville, the prime minister. Ironically, Rev. John Newton, the former slave ship captain turned evangelical Anglican priest, whose tract *Thoughts upon the African Slave Trade* gave impetus to a 20-year crusade to end the Atlantic slave trade, died a few months later in December 1807. As now celebrated in the film *Amazing Grace*, which came out in February 2007, one of the most effective voices championing abolition of the slave trade was that of the Tory MP William Wilberforce, a young friend of Newton. Romantic cinematographic fiction aside (e.g., Newton's poem "Amazing Grace" was put to the now-universally-recognized tune "Loving Lambs" only in the 1830s and in the United States, not England, and therefore could not have been sung at the wedding of Wilberforce and Barbara Spooner in 1797), the film does a good job of showing the ultimately successful work of the Society for the Abolition of the Slave Trade and the dedication of such luminaries as Wilberforce, Thomas Clarkson, Olaudah Equiano, Hannah More, Charles Fox, and John Newton. It also does a better than average job of showing how the slave trade interests of Liverpool, represented forcefully by Banastre Tarleton, slowly but almost inexorably surrendered the high ground to the moral arguments of Wilberforce and his associates, many of whom were Quakers and Methodists. It does less of a good job at showing the ambiguities, contradictions, and imperfections within this crusade and its saintly crusaders. Newton had continued in the slave trade for six years after his conversion to evangelical Christianity in 1748, and in a pamphlet of 1807, Wilberforce argued that immediate emancipation would be ruinous for the slaves, who needed a substantial period of indentured training and education before freedom. Moreover, the 1807 act did not totally end the careers of British slave traders. It stipulated a fine of £100 for each slave found on a British ship. The fine was potentially ruinous, but potential profits were such that some masters and owners continued in the trade under the understanding that if they were sighted by a British man-of-war they would drown their cargo before boarding and discovery.

However less than perfect the act and the all-too-human but idealistic people who carried it through Parliament were, it and they set in motion a movement that could not be stopped. Unlike the United States' version, this act of 1807 was the first step toward an essentially peaceful eradication of African slavery as a legal institution in Great Britain and throughout most of its possessions. In July 1833, the Abolition of Slavery Act passed the House of Commons. Although it exempted Ceylon, Saint Helena, and lands governed by the Honourable East India Company and provided for a substantial period of semi-free "apprenticeship" for freed slaves, it was sweeping and revolutionary. Yet, its setting aside a fund of £20,000,000 as compensation for former slave-owners also points out the conservative forces behind this great revolution. Only days later, Wilberforce died, his life's work accomplished. Hannah More, his former associate in the fight against the slave trade, died that same year, as also did his former rival in Parliament, Banastre Tarleton.

Great Britain's eventual abolition of slavery and its consequent attempt to end the commerce in humans that had for so long been the shame of the transatlantic world was an important first step in the eventual prohibition of slavery throughout much of the world by the end of the nineteenth century, however slow and tentative its first steps must have seemed to the zealots who led the charge against it. The campaign against human bondage continued into the 20th century and was embraced by the League of Nations and its successor, the United Nations. Yet, despite all of this, the curse of slavery persists. The London-based Society for the Abolition of the Slave Trade has metamorphosed into Anti-Slavery International, which vigorously continues the battle against forced human labor. According to its estimates, some 12 million humans, a large percentage of them children, are today subject to bondage of some form or other, most of it illegal but much of it socially tolerated. Apparently no region of the world is free of this evil, including Great Britain and the United States, where undocumented immigrants are especially vulnerable.

As I ruminate on all of this, I sit in my study in Burlington, Vermont. Vermont proudly claims to be the first polity in North America to ban slavery by written constitution, when the Commonwealth of

Vermont declared itself an independent republic in 1777, and it was the first state in the Union to prohibit the servitude of adult humans when it became the fourteenth state in 1791. And yet evidence suggests strongly that there were a handful of adult slaves in Vermont after 1777 and probably after 1791. Moreover, the prohibition did not extend to male children under the age of 21 or female children under 18, thereby leaving open the possibility of indentured minors. For all of this, Vermont shed more blood per capita than any other Union state in the Civil War, and much of that blood was shed by persons who saw it as a war for freedom and to end the blight of slavery—a blight that was ended by law, but not totally in fact, in 1865.

Ironies, ambiguities, and contradictions are inherent in the human condition and do not shock or surprise the historian. They certainly do not surprise Lisa Lindsay, the author of this important, disturbing, yet ultimately triumphant study—a book that records in great detail not only one of the most shameful episodes in human history, the trade in and exploitation of African slaves in the New World, but also one of Western civilization's greatest accomplishments, the end of legal slavery. That abolition was, at times, slow in coming, and it was more often than not painfully imperfect in execution, as contemporary social, economic, and political problems bear witness in all the countries in the Western Hemisphere that experienced African slavery.

Captives as Commodities deals with tragedy and triumph, yet in no way is this book either an unalloyed litany of indictments or a piece of triumphalist rhetoric. Rather, it is a carefully nuanced work that reflects both the most up-to-date scholarship on this complex issue and the subtlety of mind of a first-rate historian. To be sure, Lindsay writes with passion and is not afraid to point out the inarguable inhumanities that African slaves suffered at all stages of their captivity and exploitation. There is no glossing over evil here. But at the same time, she shows how African states and chiefdoms were complicit in this awful trade. In short, the balance, fair-mindedness, and exacting scholarship that underpin this book exhibit, not by word but by example, the fact that good historical scholarship must come to grips with ambiguities, contradictions, and the gray tones of reality. History is not black and white, not even the history of the enslavement and abuse of Africans for the profit of Europeans and Euro-Americans.

The instructors and students who use this book as a course text will come away enriched. They will have had the pleasure of reading the best available survey of this phenomenon in an easily readable format. They will also have experienced the challenge of struggling with evidentiary data—primary sources, illustrations, and charts—that they are asked to analyze, and, on the basis of that analysis, of answering some rather unsettling but important questions. Beyond that, they will have had the uncomfortable but intellectually necessary experience of having had many of their preconceptions challenged. That, after all, is the beginning of true understanding. Put bluntly, how and why humans were transformed into commodities in the not-so-distant past and, equally, how and why the modern West came to repudiate this practice is a story that each of us has an obligation to know and understand.

Alfred J. Andrea
Series Editor

About the Author

Lisa A. Lindsay holds a Ph.D. in African history from the University of Michigan and teaches at the University of North Carolina at Chapel Hill. Before developing her scholarship on the slave trade, she published *Working with Gender: Wage Labor and Social Change in Southwestern Nigeria*, *Men and Masculinities in Modern Africa* (co-edited with Stephan F. Miescher), and scholarly articles on colonial Nigeria. She has held fellowships from the American Council of Learned Societies, the National Humanities Center, and the National Endowment for the Humanities.

Acknowledgments

In spite of its horrific subject matter and inescapably academic format, this book was (mostly) pleasant to write; and for that I thank all the people who helped and encouraged me. Jonathan Reynolds originally suggested that I write this book—I owe him either a beer or a knuckle sandwich. Al Andrea wasn't kidding when he said that he would be an active editor, and I'm grateful for his expertise, great ideas, and good humor. I couldn't ask for a more supportive editor at Prentice Hall than Charles Cavaliere. My colleagues at UNC-Chapel Hill, led by the witty and wise Lloyd Kramer, have generously looked the other way as I've written this, since I was supposed to be working on something else. John Chasteen kindly gave me a last-minute lesson in Brazilian history. All-star historian Joe Miller read the manuscript in its final stages, generously providing help on issues large and small. I also thank David Eltis for sharing with me information from the forthcoming second edition of the Transatlantic Slave Trade Database.

For the past six years, I've taught an undergraduate lecture course on the Atlantic slave trade at UNC. I'm grateful to all the teaching assistants—Dave Carlson, Joy Jackson, Bill Van Norman, Oscar Chamosa, Amos Esty, Amy Crow, Tomoko Yagyu, Elizabeth Gritter, Josh Nadel, Enver Casimir, Kim Hill, Toby Nathan, Matt Harper, Maren Wood, Hilary Green, and Eliot Spencer—who have saved me from embarrassing gaffes, filled in the considerable gaps in my knowledge, shown me how to convey ideas to students, and (occasionally) tolerated my long-winded stories and marginally successful jokes. I also thank Dave Carlson, who read the initial book proposal and offered helpful suggestions, and Julia Osman, who provided the picture from *Candide.* The students in History 78/278 get high marks (sometimes even literally) for their deep engagement, earnest sense of inquiry, and generous spirit.

Jay Kaufman, Jolie Olcott, Cara Robertson, Pete Sigal, Luise White, and my parents Dianne Lindsay and Wendell Lindsay have probably heard as much about this book as they can stand. Thank you for your patience, and for encouraging me to keep writing. Thanks, also, to Cara for the talking Mr. T toy, which is always a good motivator. John Wood Sweet has become my African history buddy as well as my friend, and I'm grateful for the ideas, sources, laughs, and tasty meals he continues to feed me. As I was writing this book, Tim Tyson read every word—and rearranged many of them, too. I appreciate his warmth and generosity, as well as his literary talents.

Writing about people torn away from their loved ones has reminded me once again to count my blessings. My children Amelia (a.k.a."Oatmeal") and Julian Lindsay-Kaufman top the list. I thank them for helping with this book only indirectly—by bringing me joy every day.

Lisa A. Lindsay

Introduction

THE SLAVE TRADE AND THE WESTERN WORLD

This book centers on one of the most tragic, horrifying, and important pieces of the history of the Western world: the transatlantic slave trade. Between the early 1500s and the latter 1800s, millions of captive African men, women, and children were forcibly marched to the coast, crowded into rancid sailing ships, barely kept alive as they traveled across the Atlantic, and disembarked on a new continent to work in brutal conditions largely among strangers. The bodies of more than a million of them—casualties of the horrific crossing—decomposed in the Atlantic Ocean. The survivors and their descendants were compelled to give their lives building the physical, economic, and cultural features of the American South, the West Indies, Brazil, and other parts of South America. Profits from their labors supported elites in the Americas and Europe and fueled regional and national economic development. For generations, the slave trade was the major impetus for contact between

Europe and Africa—a relationship that ultimately included colonialism and underdevelopment. In the Western world, modern ideologies about race largely originated with the slave trade. This massive system of commerce was foundational to the development of the world as we know it.

Unlike any other system of commerce in world history, the primary commodities exchanged in the slave trade were people, and this fact has implications not only for how the trade was initiated, conducted, conceptualized, and concluded, but also for how we make sense of it in the present. For on one hand, the Atlantic slave trade was indeed *trade,* and as such it bears comparison with and was related to the expansion of a variety of global commercial networks.[1] Shocking as this may seem today, most Europeans involved in the slave trade conceived of Africans as physically comparable to other trade goods. Indeed, their commercial inventories, shipping lists, and tax records have provided modern historians with valuable source material. On the other hand, unlike sugar, salt, spices, and textiles—other commodities driving cross-cultural exchange in world history—slaves were human, with all this implies about their vulnerability to pain and discomfort, their capacity to resist, their real or potential relationships with sellers and buyers, and—most fundamentally to those sellers and buyers—their labor power. Understanding the Atlantic slave trade thus requires studying economic and political history, dealing largely with those who bought and sold slaves, as well as the social and cultural history of slavers, the enslaved, and the societies they lived in and built.

WAYS OF STUDYING THE SLAVE TRADE

Examined at the level of individual captives, the slave trade represents human tragedy. This was the emphasis of many of the early works on the history of the slave trade, which were generated by abolitionists and drew on testimony from former participants. Intended to sway public opinion against the trade, these accounts emphasized its inhumanity and brutal effects on individuals. The abolitionist tradition has continued to influence scholars interested in the slave trade, but they

---

[1]See Erik Gilbert and Jonathan Reynolds's Connections Series book *Trading Tastes: Commodity and Cultural Exchange to 1750* (Pearson Prentice Hall, 2006).

have also turned their attention to the overall contours of the trade and its large-scale ramifications. One influential line of inquiry, initiated in the 1940s by the West Indian historian Eric Williams, focused on the slave trade's economic importance, particularly in Britain. As is discussed later in this book, Williams argued that profits from slavery and the slave trade contributed to the development of British capitalism, an economic system which in turn ultimately brought about slavery's demise. Other historians have concentrated on the economic, political, and demographic effects of the slave trade on African societies, both on a regional scale and in particular times in history. The Guyanese scholar Walter Rodney argued in his influential book *How Europe Underdeveloped Africa* (1972), for instance, that the slave trade and colonialism systematically damaged African societies as they enriched Europe.

Understanding the aggregate effects of the slave trade requires solid information about its overall volume and structure. Until the mid-20th century, estimates of the numbers of enslaved Africans brought to the New World were based on ideologically influenced guesses. Then, the historian Philip Curtin determined to answer the question of how many slaves were transported from Africa to the Americas in a more systematic way. His influential book *The Atlantic Slave Trade: A Census*, published in 1969 and based largely on the shipping and commercial records then available, asserted a figure which was lower than common estimates at the time. The ensuing controversy prompted new research, including a massive database compiled by scholars at Harvard University's DuBois Institute. *The Trans-Atlantic Slave Trade: A Database on CD-ROM*, published in 1999, represents an international, collaborative effort to bring together all the information available on voyages associated with the Atlantic slave trade. The database has been further updated, and a second edition will be posted on the Internet in 2008.[2] Containing information on 34,850 voyages between 1519 and 1867, the revised database, like the CD-ROM version, will list individual ships' names, captains, and owners, as well as where they picked up

---

[2]David Eltis, Stephen D. Behrendt, David Richardson, and Herbert S. Klein (eds.), *The Trans-Atlantic Slave Trade: A Database on CD-ROM* (Cambridge: Cambridge University Press, 1999), revised as David Eltis, Stephen D. Behrendt, David Richardson, and Manolo Florentino (eds.), *The Transatlantic Slave Trade: An Enhanced and On-line Database* (forthcoming in 2008).

slaves, where they disembarked, and additional information.[3] A major scholarly advance, the database makes possible much more precise accounting than ever before of the overall numbers of people and ships involved in the trade, and changes in the trade over time and space.

OVERVIEW OF THE ATLANTIC SLAVE TRADE

The Atlantic slave trade was a humanitarian catastrophe on an enormous scale. Nearly four times as many enslaved Africans crossed the Atlantic Ocean before 1820 as did Europeans. According to the most recent computations based on the revised slave trade database, approximately 12.5 million captives embarked from Africa, of which 10.8 million made it alive to the Americas. The difference in figures represents deaths during the Middle Passage. Approximately one-third of the captives were women, and 28 percent were children. The transatlantic trade spanned more than 300 years, from the 16th through the 19th centuries, with the majority of captives—some 6.4 million— shipped between 1700 and 1800. Nearly 4 million, or almost a third of the total, were transported in the second half of the 18th century alone. In contrast, about 2.1 million Africans were taken to the Americas over the first 200 years of the trade. Stunningly, over 3 million Africans were taken as slaves to the Americas even after Britain (the major slave trading power at the time) outlawed its citizens' participation in the trade as of 1808.

Many European nations were involved in the slave trade, including Portugal, Spain, Britain, France, the Netherlands, Denmark, Brazil, and the United States. As Figure I.1 indicates, Portuguese traders dominated Atlantic slaving before 1726 and after 1807, while the British were the leading carriers in between, during the peak period of the slave trade.

---

[3]The revised dataset is estimated to include nearly 80 percent of all transatlantic slaving voyages ever attempted. Its greatest gaps are for the 16th and 17th centuries. In contrast, it likely includes over 95 percent of the voyages undertaken between 1700 and 1825, by far the peak period of the slave trade. Wherever possible, statistics presented in this book are from the revised version of the database as summarized in David Eltis and David Richardson (eds.), "Introduction," in *Extending the Frontiers: Essays on the New Transatlantic Slave Trade Database* (Yale University Press, forthcoming). I thank David Eltis for sharing this with me. Other statistics are from the 1999 edition.

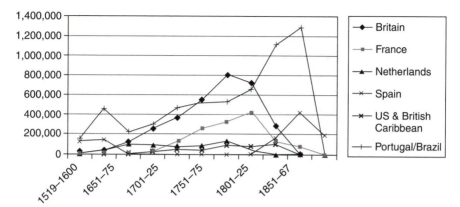

FIGURE I.1   Volume of the Transatlantic Slave Trade by Nationality of carrier[4]

Portuguese and Brazilian vessels accounted for a staggering 46 percent of all Atlantic slave-trading voyages, with British ships comprising 25 percent and French, 11 percent. Spanish ships supplied slaves to Spain's colonies in the early and late years of the slave trade, but during the peak years of the trade, relatively few captives were transported under the Spanish flag. Instead, the Spanish government relied on foreign firms to supply its territories under a licensing system called the *asiento*. The territory that became the United States was supplied mainly by British traders, although in the late colonial and early national periods, there were some U.S.-based international slave merchants.

As Figure I.2 shows, most enslaved Africans were not transported to North America, in spite of its large enslaved population by the 19th century. In fact, the territory that became the United States received less than 4 percent of the total number of captive Africans. More than 40 percent of the total were taken to Brazil, while the British, French, and Spanish colonies of the Caribbean together accounted for more than another 40 percent of the total volume. Given the dominance of the Portuguese and British slave trades, it follows that Brazil and British America received most Africans. The British colonies of the Americas (including North America and the Caribbean together) brought in about one-fourth of the total number

[4]Created from data in the Transatlantic Slave Trade Database, 2nd edition (hereafter "TSTD2"), as reported in Table 2 of David Eltis' unpublished paper, "The Transatlantic Slave Trade: A Reassessment Based on the Second Edition of the Transatlantic Slave Trade Database." I am grateful to Joseph C. Miller for sharing this paper with me.

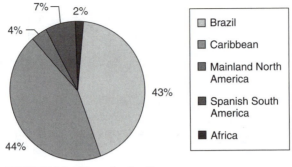

FIGURE I.2   Slave destinations

of captive African imports. Another 7 percent went to the Spanish South American mainland.

The large proportion of African slaves who ended their lives in the Caribbean and northeastern Brazil reflects the importance of sugar plantations, or the economies that supported them, in creating demand for slaves. The vast majority of captives were brought to the Americas because of sugar. Yet, in the earliest years of the transatlantic slave trade, Africans were transported principally to Mexico and Peru, where they worked in mining, agriculture, and urban services. Northeastern Brazil became the first major sugar exporting area of the New World in the 16th century, when Native American slaves began to be replaced by Africans. Sugar production and African slavery expanded with Dutch, British, and French colonization in the West Indies, beginning in the mid-1600s. Huge and numerous sugar plantations, along with estates growing other crops like coffee, were developed on British Jamaica and French St. Domingue (Haiti) in the 1700s. In the late 1700s Spanish settlers developed slave-worked sugar plantations on Cuba, the colony that replaced St. Domingue as the world's primary sugar producer after the Haitian Revolution. Cuba's planters also put enslaved Africans to work in coffee production and a variety of other occupations. In North America, and in Brazil as well, African slavery was not always correlated with sugar. In British North America and the early United States, Africans grew a variety of crops including tobacco, rice, and indigo; in the 19th century their descendants often concentrated on producing cotton. With a slave population of nearly a million in 1800, Brazil had the largest single concentration of slaves with the

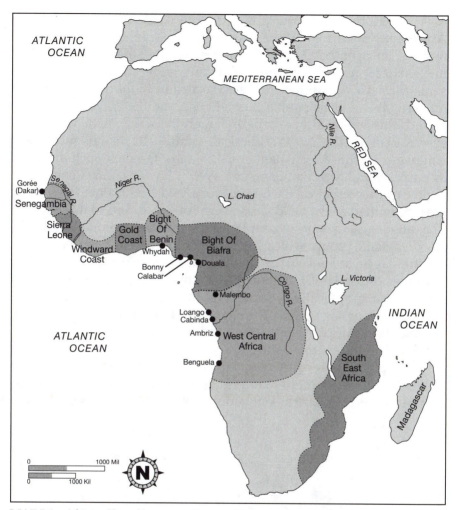

MAP I.1   African Slave-Exporting Regions

Source: "New Perspectives on the Transatlantic Slave Trade," Special Issue, *William and Mary Quarterly*, 58 (2001): 16–17.

widest range of jobs, including sugar and coffee cultivation, mining, and work in urban industries.

Captive Africans came from the eight regions identified on Map I.1: Senegambia, Sierra Leone, the Windward Coast (modern-day Liberia and the Ivory Coast), the Gold Coast (now Ghana), the Bight of Benin (coastal Togo, Republic of Benin, and southwestern Nigeria), the

Bight of Biafra (southeastern Nigeria and Cameroon), West Central Africa, and Southeast Africa. (A "bight" is a bend in the coastline forming an open bay.) These eight regions are sometimes collapsed into three larger ones, whose inhabitants each share some cultural similarities. Upper Guinea includes the area from the Senegal River to modern Liberia (Senegambia, Sierra Leone, and the Windward Coast). Inland, this region's landscape is largely savanna, with wide-open spaces akin to the North American prairie. Its inhabitants speak languages in the West Atlantic and Mande families, including, for example, Mandinka, Bambara, and Wolof. Lower Guinea entails the region from present-day western Ivory Coast to Cameroon, or the areas identified as the Gold Coast, Bight of Benin, and Bight of Biafra. The languages spoken by people in this forested region fall into the Kwa language group, which is divided into Akan and Aja languages (the former includes Twi, the language of Asante; Yoruba and Fon are examples of the latter). Although the Angola coast, or West Central Africa, is geographically very large, its inhabitants speak related Western Bantu languages, like KiKongo, Kimbundu, and Ovimbundu. West Central Africa's landscape is tropical forest, with savanna, or grassland, to the south.

Although more captives came from West Africa (Upper and Lower Guinea combined) than West Central Africa, Figure I.3 shows that West Central Africa sent more captives to the Americas than

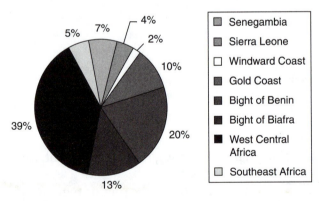

Upper Guinea: 13%
Lower Guinea: 43%
West Central Africa: 39%
Southeast Africa: 5%

FIGURE I.3   Origins of African slaves

any other single region. West Central Africa's dominance was most pronounced during the first 150 years of the transatlantic slave trade, when more than two out of three slaves came from West Central Africa, and again in the 19th century. For a century at the beginning and a quarter century at the end of the trade, West Central Africa sent more slaves than all other African regions combined. Overall, 39 percent of enslaved Africans came from this region. The Bight of Benin was the major region of slave departure between 1676 and 1725, and overall it took second place, with 20 percent of all embarked slaves. This volume, combined with substantial slave exports from the Bight of Biafra (13 percent of the total) and the Gold Coast (10 percent), made Lower Guinea a major source of captives. Upper Guinea, although geographically closest to Europe and North America, supplied the fewest slaves (a curious point that will be probed further in Chapter 3). Southeast Africa became an important sending area only in the early 19th century, when slavers responded to British-led efforts to suppress the Atlantic slave trade in part by seeking new sources of supply outside of established networks; still, the region supplied only about 5 percent of the overall total.

CONNECTIONS

While the numerical data give us a good sense of *what happened*, or rather, of which people were moved where by which people, they do not address questions of *why* or *how*. After providing some background information in the remainder of the Introduction, this book will address a series of such questions. Why did Europeans buy African slaves? Why did (some) African societies sell slaves? How did enslaved people respond, endure, resist, and help to make American culture? How did the Atlantic slave trade finally come to an end? In a fairly chronological structure, *Captives as Commodities* traces the origins, expansion, and decline of the transatlantic trade in addition to its impact on the Americas, Africa, and Europe. The Atlantic slave trade lasted more than 300 years and connected people, goods, and ideas across four continents. In addition to slavers and the enslaved, it directly or indirectly involved thousands of people ranging from European and American business- men and bankers who financed the trade, to manufacturers and ship-builders who provided the necessary equipment, to farmers in Africa who sold their agricultural surpluses to feed the captives awaiting export on the coast. This book is intended to help students and other readers understand the complex web of connections that linked together the lives and fates of various Africans, Europeans, and Americans via the Atlantic slave trade.

THE OLD WORLD BACKGROUND TO NEW WORLD SLAVERY

In the year 73 BCE, in the Roman town of Capua, 78 gladiators began what became the Roman Empire's largest and deadliest slave revolt. These enslaved men were being trained to fight to the death for the amusement of spectators. Under the leadership of Spartacus, a slave who had been born into a nomadic tribe in Thrace (present-day Bulgaria) and captured in battle by the Roman army, they broke out of the gladiator school and fled to Mount Vesuvius. There, Spartacus raised a rebel army that swelled to perhaps 70,000 escaped slaves. Over the next two years, Spartacus's forces marched first north to Gaul and then south toward Sicily, defeating at least seven Roman legions sent to crush them. Along the way, they accumulated not only able-bodied male followers but also women, children, and elderly men. In 71 BCE, three combined Roman armies finally defeated the rebels. After Spartacus and thousands of his followers were killed in battle, the Romans crucified approximately 6,000 others along the Via Appia from Capua to Rome.

Spartacus's story illustrates two main themes that provide an important background for understanding the Atlantic slave trade. First, slavery was a very old, accepted institution until relatively recently in world history. It was featured in the Jewish and Christian portions of the Bible and the writings of Aristotle, Islamic religious law, Hindu sacred texts, and Chinese tradition, to take just a few examples. In many ways, Spartacus's status was not unlike that of slaves in, say, the 18th-century Caribbean or 19th-century U.S. South. He was considered to be property, or chattel, meaning that his person could be bought and sold. His masters could coerce him at will through violence or threats. His labor power was at the complete disposal of a master; and though he was employed in a particular occupation (grisly entertainment), as a slave he could be put to any task in the economy.

Second, Spartacus's story reminds us that our modern associations between slavery and "race" have a fairly shallow history. On one hand, slavery has always been based on defining people as outsiders, either by capture and transportation or through judicial processes stripping them of their membership in the community. Spartacus was a war captive, taken from a place where he spoke the language, enjoyed kinship and social bonds, shared the prevailing culture, and understood the political system to a new milieu where he was completely alienated. In ancient Rome as elsewhere in the premodern world, enslaved outsiders had diverse origins; there was no rigid association between "race" (a term that took its modern meaning relatively recently) and slavery. In fact, as enslaved people or their descendants assimilated to the dominant society and became less foreign, their status could improve, even to the point of becoming free. In contrast, even though manumission (setting a slave free) was possible in the New World, for the overwhelming majority of slaves in the Americas, their children and grandchildren could expect to inherit their unfree status simply on the basis of their skin color and ascribed "race."

Although the institution of slavery has existed as long as anyone knows, until the plantation societies of the Americas, it largely coexisted with other forms of unfree or quasi-free labor. Most communities where slavery existed were *societies with slaves,* that is, they included slavery but the economic, political, and social systems did not rest upon it. In contrast, the Roman Empire, like the plantation Americas, is considered to have been a *slave society,* where slavery was a fundamental organizing principle. At the height of Roman Empire, Italy contained an estimated 2–3 million slaves, representing 35–40 percent of the total population. As in later plantation societies, the Roman Empire featured a regularized system of supplying slaves (in this case, military conquest and expansion), a wealthy class that could pay to own slaves, an economic system in which elite landowners used slave labor to produce agricultural crops for sale, and a legal system that recognized slavery. "Slaves are in the power of their masters, and this power is derived from the law of nations," according to a compilation of imperial Roman law commissioned by Emperor Justinian (r. 527–565), "for we find that among all nations masters have the power of life and death over their slaves, and whatever a slave earns belongs to his master." But as in the plantation societies of the Americas, slaves resisted their status and conditions.

Spartacus's uprising was the third major slave revolt in the Roman Empire.

Slaves did not disappear from Europe until well into the modern period, but slavery as a major economic institution collapsed with the barbarian invasions that ended the western half of the Roman Empire between the late 4th and 6th centuries CE. As urban markets declined, long-distance trade broke down, and agricultural estates became increasingly self-sufficient, slave labor was no longer available and economically efficient. At the time of England's Domesday Book, a census held in 1086, slaves were reported to comprise as much as one-tenth of England's population, but the proportion dropped sharply from that point on. Most agricultural labor came to be performed by serfs (so-called semifree agricultural laborers who were bound to the land but enjoyed certain rights of freedom), while some wealthy nobles kept a few slaves as household servants and status symbols. The politically fragmented Slavic lands between the eastern Adriatic and Black Seas became a major source of supply for the European slave trading that did go on, primarily conducted by Viking and Italian traders. In fact, the term *slave* in all West European languages derives from *Slav*. (In Medieval Latin *sclavus* meant both Slav and slave.)

Meanwhile, slavery also existed in the Islamic world. Although slavery pre-dated Islam in Arabia, the holy wars that spread Islam from Arabia throughout the Persian Gulf region and across North Africa beginning in the 7th century created new sources of captives. Non-Muslim outsiders were considered to be enslavable, giving slavery a religious justification. (Jews and Christians, as "People of the Book," were theoretically not subject to enslavement under Muslim laws, although in practice they could be enslaved, especially when captured in battle.) As in the Roman Empire, Muslim societies used slaves in economic production, the military (as *mamluks*, or slave soldiers), administration, and domestic service. Since slaves were often freed after their conversion to Islam, and because the offspring of slave women and Muslim men were born free, Islamic slavery was generally not hereditary. Slave labor instead came from a constant flow of captives into Islamic territory from conquered lands in Central Asia and Africa, and through trade.

The Muslim conquest of North Africa gave Islamic masters access to slaves from south of the Sahara. Trade across the Sahara Desert has gone on as long as anyone knows, although it expanded with the introduction of dromedaries (single-humped camels) in the first half of the first millennium CE. Caravans from North Africa, together with members of trading diaspora communities from farther south, exchanged salt, gold, horses, and other commodities at oasis trading posts. Beginning in the 8th century, Islamic merchants purchased African slaves who had traveled these routes, as well as others supplied through a maritime trade on the East African coast. In fact, by 869 CE, Arabs had transported enough black slaves from East Africa to the Persian Gulf to ignite an extensive revolt in what is now Iraq. The so-called Zanj slaves had been working in regimented gangs to reclaim abandoned marshland, remove mineral deposits, and prepare the soil for cultivation. They killed thousands of Arab men, enslaved countless women and children, and even threatened Baghdad before they were finally crushed in 883, 14 years after the revolt began. Although large-scale gang slavery declined after the revolt, African slaves continued to toil in Muslim lands. North African traders supplied a steady stream of African captives from across the Sahara, approximately 5,000 per year between the 10th and 15th centuries.

The Muslim injunction against enslaving fellow believers had its counterpart in the Christian kingdoms of Western Europe (and Byzantium as well). Muslim armies overran most of the Iberian Peninsula in the early 8th century and even encroached upon southern France. This threat, combined with the declining importance of slavery overall in medieval Europe, contributed to a new doctrine, attributed to Charlemagne, that Christians should not enslave other Christians. But such a prohibition was contested and generally ignored, largely because political disintegration meant that there was no centralized authority to regulate slave trading. It was only during the European kingdoms' renewed clashes with Islam during the Crusades (late 11th–late 16th centuries) that the unofficial ban on selling or holding most fellow Christians as slaves was revived.

The Crusades were also significant for the history of the slave trade because they introduced Europeans to sugar cultivation, which would become the *raison d'être* of most plantation economies of the Americas. Tiny, precious bits of cane sugar from the Levant and North Africa had occasionally appeared in Western Europe. But during the Crusades, European settlers in the Levant established their own sugar-growing estates, using slave labor. Even after the Europeans were expelled from mainland Southwest Asia in the late

13th century, they continued to produce sugar on the eastern Mediterranean island of Cyprus, and then Sicily and Crete as well, though with mixed slave and free labor forces. Their developing a taste for sugar, along with growing expertise in its cultivation, combined with European maritime advances to set the foundations for African slavery in the Americas.

THE MARITIME REVOLUTION AND EUROPEAN TRADE WITH AFRICA

In 1415, Portuguese knights crossed the Strait of Gibraltar and overran the sumptuous Moroccan city of Ceuta, a victory hailed throughout Christian Europe. An extension of the Christian armies' gradual reconquest of Portugal and Spain over the previous three and a half centuries, the invasion also offered opportunities for plunder and trade. The capture of this rich city, reportedly more splendid than many in tiny Portugal, provided the Portuguese with more information than they previously had about the caravan trade that brought gold from south of the Sahara. Although the Portuguese were not strong enough to extend their occupation beyond the Moroccan coast and tap into the gold trade directly, religious and commercial motivations continued to motivate an important member of the Ceuta expedition, Prince Henry of Portugal, as well as other pioneers of the maritime revolution.

Henry, the third son of the king of Portugal, is known to history as "the Navigator" not because he traveled much personally, but because he provided important royal sponsorship to maritime exploration. After returning from Ceuta, Henry devoted the rest of his life (until 1460) to organizing and financing voyages of discovery, with the linked aims of spreading Christianity and acquiring wealth for the Portuguese crown. His ships established permanent contact with the islands of Madeira and the Azores, where sugar production was begun under Portuguese control in the 1440s. As they settled a string of eastern Atlantic islands, the Portuguese gained both experience and staging posts for further exploration (Map I.2).[5] (Incidentally,

---

[5]For a fuller treatment of Portuguese overseas explorations and colonization, see Chapter 1 of the Connections Series book by Glenn Ames, *The Globe Encompassed: The Age of European Discovery, 1500–1700* (Pearson Prentice Hall, 2007).

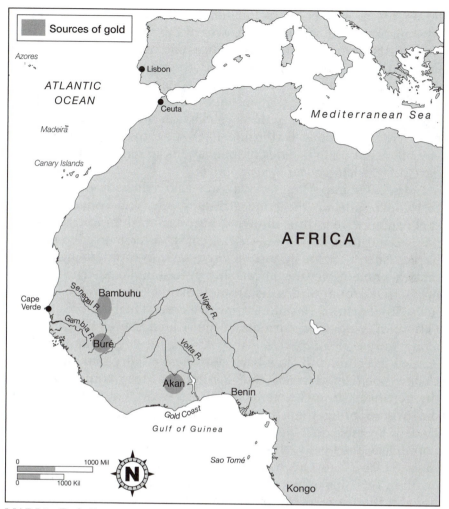

MAP I.2 Early European contacts in West Africa

Christopher Columbus spent his honeymoon on Madeira in 1478, after he married the daughter of the former Portuguese governor of the island.)

Madeira, the Canary Islands (colonized by Spanish traders from the early 1400s), and the Azores are relatively close to the Iberian Peninsula. But for European sailors to proceed farther south along the African coast, they had to confront major technological impediments. They knew, for instance, that the winds and currents of the North Atlantic both flow south along the African coast—which allowed

Europeans to sail to Africa but not to return (and also prevented Africans from sailing to Europe, even if they had wanted to). They also relied on crude navigational devices and relatively sketchy maps. During the 15th century, however, Portuguese (and later Spanish) navigators collected existing knowledge about the lands beyond Muslim North Africa and about innovations in mathematical thinking and mapmaking. They drew on classical sources, foreigners, and modern computations. By the mid-1400s their investigations began to pay off, resulting in a series of innovations so momentous that they have been called the *maritime revolution.*

The most important innovation was the development of a ship that could sail into the wind efficiently enough to overcome the pull of the current, thus allowing European sailors to travel north (i.e., home) from the West African coast. After many incremental improvements, Spanish and Portuguese ship builders created the *caravel,* a mix of Mediterranean ship design, hull construction from northern Europe, and sails from Indian Ocean Arabs. Then in the 1440s, Portuguese sailors came to a crucial realization about the pattern of winds and currents in the Atlantic: after flowing south along the northern part of West Africa, the winds and currents change direction and flow back north, essentially making a giant, clockwise circle. Mariners thus learned that they could sail out to the northwest from Africa and pick up trade winds and currents that would bring them back toward the Portuguese coast. This made it possible, in 1444, for sailors to reach the well-watered and populated lands below the Sahara, beginning at what they named Cape Verde ("the Green Cape"). By the time of Prince Henry's death in 1460, his explorers had established a secure base of operations in the Cape Verde Islands and explored 600 miles of coast farther south, as far as what they named *Sierra Leone* (a "Lion Mountain"). From there they knew the coast curved sharply to the east.

In the 1460s, the previously uninhabited Cape Verde Islands became the first base for European trading operations in sub-Saharan Africa. From there Portuguese maritime entrepreneurs hoped to finance their expeditions by tapping into the African gold trade and, secondarily, procuring some slaves for sale. For centuries, camel caravans had brought the gold from African-controlled mines near the headwaters of the Senegal and Niger Rivers and the interior of what is now Ghana across the Sahara in exchange for the desert salt that sub-Saharan Africans used to preserve food.[6] In North Africa, the gold entered Mediterranean networks, and from there it made its way all over Europe and Western Asia. Fifteenth-century Portuguese explorers hoped to bypass North African traders and establish coastal commerce directly with the African leaders who controlled the mines, and the Cape Verde Islands offered proximity to the Senegal River trade. Additionally, they thought they might procure some African slaves for sale in Europe, where some elites still held slaves as domestic servants and exotic status symbols.

Initially, Portuguese forces raided and attempted to seize slaves and plunder along the coast. One of the first expeditions to the Senegal River, led by Lançarote de Lagos in 1444, brutally kidnapped 235 residents of several offshore islands and brought them back to Portugal for sale. Other expeditions followed this example, but soon African naval forces began to offer resistance. In 1446, Africans in canoes prevented a ship under Nuno Tristão from landing an armed force in Senegambia, killing nearly all the raiders. The next year a Danish sailor in Portuguese service named Valarte was killed along with most of his crew when local craft attacked him near the island of Gorée. As a result of such resistance, the Portuguese generally moved from raiding to peaceful trade, a pattern that continued through almost the entire history of the slave trade.

In 1456, the Portuguese crown dispatched Diogo Gomes to negotiate treaties of peace and trade with coastal African rulers. The lower Gambia River was already important in West African regional trade, and there were already some slaves available for sale. The Portuguese began to buy there, although the numbers were relatively small before 1500: perhaps 1,300 a year exported to Europe and another 500 a year to the Atlantic islands now governed by Portugal. This early European slave trade was even sanctioned by the highest order in Christian Europe: between 1442 and 1456, a series of papal bulls granted Prince Henry a monopoly on colonizing the Atlantic islands, establishing trading posts on the African coast, and taking infidels as captives.

Although it had taken the Portuguese four decades to cover the 1,500 miles from Lisbon to Sierra Leone, it took only 30 years to explore the remaining 4,000 miles to the southern tip of the African continent. After Prince Henry's death, the Portuguese crown continued to sponsor voyages of exploration, but the quickening pace resulted largely from

---

[6]For coverage of the African salt trade, see Gilbert and Reynolds, *Trading Tastes*, pp. 64–75.

the growing participation of private commercial interests. In 1469 a prominent Lisbon merchant named Fernão Gomes purchased from the crown the privilege of exploring 400 miles of coastline a year for five years in return for a monopoly on the trade he developed there. During the period of his contract, Gomes's sailors discovered an uninhabited island along the equator that they named São Tomé. Within a couple of decades, the sugar planters of Madeira had begun operations there, using enslaved Africans as a labor force. Gomes also explored what later Europeans called the Gold Coast, an area that became the focus of Portugal's West African trade.

Gomes's agents first visited the coast of what is now Ghana in 1471 and realized that this was the location from which they could best attempt to tap into the gold trade from the Akan interior. Miners in the hinterland had long sold their gold to African traders who took it to the trading cities along the southern fringe of the Sahara, where it was transferred to traders who had crossed the desert from North Africa. Recognizing that they could get more favorable terms from the Europeans, coastal Africans negotiated with a representative of King João II of Portugal, who arrived in 1482 seeking permission to erect a trading fort. One of the officers in the negotiating party was the young Christopher Columbus, who had entered Portuguese service in 1476. The visitors dressed in their best clothes, erected a reception platform, celebrated a Catholic mass, and signaled the start of negotiations with trumpets, tambourines, and drums. The African king, whose name the Portuguese rendered as "Caramansa" (perhaps "Kwamin Ansa," that is, King Ansa), staged his entrance with equal ceremony, arriving with a large group of attendants and musicians. Through an African interpreter, the two leaders exchanged flowery speeches pledging goodwill and mutual benefit. Caramansa then gave his permission for a small trading fort to be built, warning that if the Portuguese failed to be honest and peaceful traders, he and his people would move away, depriving the post of food and trade. From this trading post, named São Jorge da Mina (Saint George of the Mine), the Portuguese crown was soon purchasing gold equal to 10 percent of the world's production at the time, in return for which Africans received large quantities of goods that Portuguese ships brought from Asia, Europe, and other parts of Africa. West African gold, in fact, financed Vasco da Gama's 1497–99 voyage around the Cape of Good Hope to India. By about 1500 a caravel loaded with gold was leaving Elmina (as the name is now rendered) every month, and the Portuguese had established a string of smaller forts on the Gold Coast as well. Through the first 20 years of the 16th century, Portuguese traders purchased nearly one-fourth of all West African annual gold production.

These days Elmina is an important destination for the heritage tours that Americans take to West Africa, and its crumbling mass often features in visual representations of the slave trade. But while Elmina did ultimately become an important port of embarkation for thousands of enslaved prisoners, for the first two centuries of its operations it was primarily a trading center for minerals, as its name, "the mine," indicates. In fact, the Portuguese entered the coastal slave trade in order to buy West African gold. As they explored farther down the African coast, they began to trade goods for slaves, whom they then brought to the Gold Coast to exchange for gold. The African societies there *bought* slaves from Portuguese traders, in part to mine gold and in part to clear the forest for agriculture and state expansion. From 1475 to 1540, more than 12,000 slaves were *imported* into the Gold Coast by the Portuguese, who also shipped cloth and other goods from one part of the African coast to another.

One source for these captives and textiles was the kingdom of Benin, farther east from the Gold Coast near the Niger Delta, which Portuguese explorers reached in the 1470s. Founded some 500 years previously, the kingdom was economically vibrant, politically stable, and militarily expansive when Portuguese explorers first encountered it. Benin's Edo-speaking *oba* (king) presided over an elaborate bureaucracy from a spacious palace in the large capital city, also called Benin. In response to a Portuguese visit in 1486, the *oba* sent an ambassador to Portugal to learn more about the homeland of these strangers. Then the *oba* established a royal monopoly on Portuguese trade, selling pepper and ivory tusks as well as stone beads, textiles, and prisoners of war to be resold at Elmina. In return, Portuguese merchants provided copper and brass, fine cloths, glass beads, and a horse for the king's royal procession. Brass and copper, some from Portugal's Mediterranean and Asian trade, were used by royal craftsmen to make some of the fabulous Benin sculptures that now sit in museums or are pictured in coffee-table books (Figure I.4).

Farther along the African coast, in what is now northern Angola, Portuguese sailors encountered the kingdom of Kongo in 1482. Like the *oba* of Benin, the *manikongo* (king of Kongo) sent delegates to Portugal, established a royal monopoly on trade with the Portuguese, and expressed some interest in missionary teachings. But Kongo lacked

FIGURE I.4 Benin copper plaque from the mid-16th to 17th century, depicting a high-ranking warrior, perhaps the *oba*, flanked by musicians and a page holding a ceremonial sword. The half figures depict Portuguese traders, who brought to Benin, among other goods, the metals used to make pieces of art such as this one.

Source: "Smithsonian Institution, National Museum of African Art, accession number 82–5–3.

Benin's political stability and economic diversity. In order to help ensure the loyalty of his nobles and followers, the *manikongo* sought Portuguese allies, who could provide novel trade goods to grease the king's patronage networks. And as Portuguese allies became increasingly important in Kongo power struggles, kings committed themselves ever more to Portuguese trade, as well as to Portuguese religion and customs. King Nzinga Mbemba (Afonso), who took the Kongolese throne in 1506, made Catholicism the kingdom's official religion. Kongolese nobles adopted Portuguese titles and dress, the capital of the kingdom was renamed São Salvador, and scribes, diplomats, and some elites learned the Portuguese language. Afonso's son Henrique even was educated and ordained a priest in Portugal and served as Kongo's first bishop. To ensure a regular supply of imports and to pay for European missionaries, Kongo kings had to provide exports. But since the kingdom lacked other items the Portuguese might buy, like gold, ivory, or pepper, Kongo increasingly provided slaves, from among captives taken in war.

At first, nearly all of those unfortunate prisoners were taken either to Portugal or to the Portuguese-controlled Atlantic islands where sugar was being cultivated for a growing European market. By the late 1400s, Portuguese administrators and settlers along with Flemish and Italian merchants were developing the Azores, Madeira, the Cape Verde Islands, and São Tomé, while the Spaniards gained control over the Canary Islands. Although the Azores and Cape Verde Islands were not suited to sugar production, it became a flourishing business in Madeira, the Canaries, and São Tomé. By the 1450s, Madeira sugar was being sold on the London and Continental markets, and by the 1490s Madeira had overtaken Cyprus as a major supplier of sugar. African slaves comprised part of the labor force on all these islands, but on Madeira they toiled along with free workers from Europe, while the heterogeneous work force on the Canaries included slaves, wage earners, and—until the indigenous population became extinct—native semi-free laborers. But São Tomé, lying close to the equator just off the West Central African coast, developed from the mid-16th century into the first sugar-producing colony with plantations largely worked by enslaved Africans. By 1522 there were 60 sugar mills on São Tomé, with large planters owning up to 300 African slaves each; and over the next two decades São Tomé surpassed Madeira as the world's largest exporter of sugar.

The eastern Atlantic islands of Madeira, the Canaries, and especially São Tomé were early sites for the *plantation complex*. There, European financiers and managers oversaw the production of sugar for a European market, using African slave labor on foreign lands. This was globalization before anyone ever thought of such a term. The plantation complex had originated on the eastern Mediterranean island of Cyprus during the era of the Crusades before being carried to the Atlantic islands. From there, first Portuguese and then other European entrepreneurs would adapt the plantation model to the Americas, where it came to involve millions of doomed Africans in the most profitable collective enterprises the world had ever seen.[7]

---

[7]See also Gilbert and Reynolds, *Trading Tastes*, Chapter 3, "Sugar and Slavery."

CHAPTER 1

Why Did Europeans Buy African Slaves?

ORIGINS: ECONOMICS OR RACISM?

After being kidnapped, spirited away from his family and home, marched for six months through unfamiliar lands, and loaded onto an ocean-going ship, an 11-year-old boy fainted in terror. "When I recovered a little," he wrote many years later, "I found some black people about me.... In a little time after, amongst the poor chained men I found some of my own nation, which in a small degree gave ease to my mind. I inquired of them what was to be done with us? They gave me to understand we were to be carried to these white people's country to work for them."

With this passage in *The Interesting Narrative of Olaudah Equiano, or Gustavus Vassa, the African* (1793), the famous slave-turned-abolitionist Equiano pinpointed, through the poignant perceptions of a child, the major engine driving the forced migration of roughly 10 million Africans over four centuries: European demand for African labor.[1] Portuguese and then Dutch, British, French, Spanish, and other traders came to Africa seeking slaves, put them on European-owned and operated ships, and took them to European-owned and operated plantations in the Americas. Why were Europeans so keen to do this?

Two important preconditions, discussed already in the Introduction, form part of the answer. First, neither most Western Europeans nor any other significantly large group of people in the early modern world saw slavery as especially objectionable. Although there were relatively few slaves in early modern Europe, the institution did have a history there (as nearly everywhere) that could provide a legal, political, and ideological foundation for its expansion under new circumstances. Second, European *capabilities* were as important to the creation of the Atlantic slave trade as their aims: they began to deal in African slaves, obviously, only after they *could* do so. With new navigational information and technologies, Europeans in the late 15th century gained the ability to go to Africa and buy slaves. The whole system therefore rested on European seafaring, exploration, commerce, and colonization.

But beyond these initial preconditions, the reason Europeans created the Atlantic slave system was that their enterprises in the Americas were very profitable, and, as the young Equiano learned, their appetite for labor was voracious. As Europeans developed colonies in the Caribbean and South and North America, they established operations to mine for gold and silver; grow cash crops like tobacco, cotton or, most importantly, sugarcane; and service the growing settler populations.[2] But it was no foregone conclusion that the workers in these enterprises would be Africans, or that they would be slaves. Colonial projects made use of Native American, European, and African workers in a variety of arrangements including wage labor, indentured servitude, labor tribute (labor exacted as

---

[1]Recently, an important biographer of Equiano, Vincent Carretta, has suggested that Equiano actually was born not in Africa but in South Carolina, and that he fabricated his account of his childhood kidnapping, enslavement, and passage across the Atlantic. Other scholars dispute this claim and remain convinced that Equiano was African in origin. Regardless of whether or not Equiano was American-born, he certainly would have been familiar with true accounts of enslavement and the Middle Passage from his London-based, African associates. More information about Equiano is in Chapter 4.

[2]For a description of the labor-intensive production of refined sugar from sugarcane, see Gilbert and Reynolds, *Trading Tastes*, pp. 84–8.

a tax), and chattel slavery. African slavery expanded in different parts of the Americas through varying processes and chronologies. In general, however, Europeans purchased African slaves when cheaper or more plentiful alternatives were unavailable and when their profits were sufficient to cover the costs. In doing so, they built upon institutions and practices involving African slavery elsewhere, expanding it by bits and pieces rather than through a conscious, grand design.

Europeans thus enslaved Africans because it made economic sense (in a twisted logic that valued only labor and not human life). But the fact that slavery and African descent intertwined in the Americas might suggest that Africans were also made into slaves because of European racism. Certainly it is true that Europeans never seriously contemplated staffing their American colonies with chattel slaves from Europe, and prejudice existed well before the 16th century. But the ethnocentrism of early modern Europeans—based on demarcations of religion, language, and culture—was not the same as the more rigid racism that emerged in the Western world by the 18th century. The racial thinking that then supported slavery degraded all people of African descent, regardless of their individual attributes, and reserved freedom—with only few exceptions—for those designated as "white." Scholars generally agree that racism and African slavery developed in the Americas *together*, even if they have varying interpretations about exactly how that unfolded. The tragic history of Western racism—with all the violence and degradation that are inseparable from it—began with the slave trade.

EARLY LABOR DEMAND IN THE NEW WORLD

The voyages of discovery that led Portuguese explorers to make contact with West Africans also brought about the European "discovery" of the Americas (see Map 1.1). Explorers pushed south along the African coast in hopes of finding a passage around Africa to the rich trade of the Indian Ocean. In 1488 Bartolomeu Dias became the first European to reach the southern tip of Africa; in 1497–98 a Portuguese expedition led by Vasco da Gama sailed around Africa and reached India. As every American student knows, in 1492 a Spanish-funded expedition led by Christopher Columbus reached the islands of the Caribbean, whose inhabitants Columbus insisted on calling Indians

MAP 1.1 The Colonial Americas, ca. 1770

since he thought the islands were part of the East Indies. In 1498, two months after Vasco da Gama reached India, Columbus sighted the mainland of South America. In 1500, an expedition under Pedro Alvares Cabral, while swinging wide to the west in the South Atlantic to catch the winds that would sweep them around southern Africa and on to India, came on the eastern coast of South America, laying the basis for Portugal's claim to Brazil.

Drawing on models from Cyprus and Madeira, early Spanish colonists attempted to set up sugar plantations in their newly acquired territories. Christopher Columbus—who had spent ten years in Madeira—introduced sugarcane to Hispañola (the island on which the Dominican Republic and Haiti are now located) during his second voyage in 1493, and Spanish technicians from the Canary Islands tried again in 1503 and 1517. Little came of these efforts, largely because of lack of labor.

Columbus's efforts to establish sugar production on Hispañola coincided with the kind of population losses that would devastate the post-conquest Americas as a whole. Out of contact with the disease environment of the Old World, Native Americans' immune systems had no resistance to the great variety of infectious and parasitic diseases that had long plagued Africans, Europeans, and Asians. Smallpox, measles, whooping cough, chickenpox, and mumps, among others, swept through Native American communities with devastating effect. Smallpox, for example, first struck the Caribbean in 1518. Combined with the harsh Spanish labor regime, losses to the indigenous Taino people were catastrophic. By the 1540s, the Taino population of the Caribbean had dropped from several million to a few thousand.[3]

Aware of the African slaves who cultivated sugar on the Atlantic islands, Spanish planters sought a core group of African slaves for their Caribbean estates. West Africans brought by sea had already replaced all other ethnic and religious groups in the European slave markets by the 16th century. In 1518, Spain's King Charles I granted a special license known as an *asiento* to a member of his household, allowing for the importation of 4,000 African slaves into Spain's Caribbean possessions (Hispañola, Cuba, Jamaica, and Puerto Rico). But problems with shipping and marketing sugar back in Europe hampered the early Caribbean industry, which was soon eclipsed by the fabulously lucrative mineral production of mainland South America.

In the 16th century, the Spanish largely abandoned their enterprises in the Caribbean, concentrating instead on conquering the larger and richer territories of Meso- and South America. Between their military advantages and the help of Old World diseases, the conquistadors defeated the Aztecs of central Mexico and the Incas of Peru, as well as inhabitants of more thinly populated areas of South America by the mid-1500s. Although Portuguese settlement in the

---

[3]See Chapter 2 of the Connections Series book by John Aberth, *The First Horseman: Disease in World History* (Prentice Hall, 2006) for a study of the impact of smallpox on the Americas.

New World developed more slowly, most of the Brazilian coast was occupied before the end of the 16th century.

For the Spaniards, the discovery of vast quantities of precious metals provided both the motive and the resources for South American colonization. Spanish treasure-hunters made their first important silver strikes in Mexico in the 1530s and 1540s. Then in 1545 the single richest silver deposit in the Americas was discovered at Potosí (in Bolivia, but then part of Peru). Mexican and Peruvian silver poured into Spain, from which it proceeded throughout Europe and even to China.

In Brazil, where mineral deposits would not be exploited for another century or more, the Portuguese sought to capitalize on sugar production, which they already knew from the Atlantic islands. The Portuguese introduced sugar from Madeira to Brazil in the mid-1540s. After 1550, sugar production expanded rapidly in the northern provinces of Pernambuco and Bahia. By 1560, production there roughly equaled that of Madeira, and by 1580 it had doubled. As of the turn of the 17th century, sugar dominated the Brazilian economy.

In the early years, Spanish mining operations in Mexico and Peru as well as Portuguese sugar plantations depended on the labor of Native Americans. Native populations were already there where the labor was needed, and they could be coerced because of the substantial technological and military advantages Europeans held over them. But everywhere, would-be planters, mine-operators, and other employers (or exploiters) faced the same problem: massive population losses brought on by European conquest. Although precise population statistics do not exist, the estimates are staggering. In the century following Cortés's defeat of the Aztecs in 1521, the population of central Mexico is thought to have fallen from somewhere between 13 and 25 million to approximately 700,000, and to the south, in the Yucatan and beyond, nearly 75 percent of the Maya population died. In the region of the Inca Empire, the population fell from about 9 million to approximately 600,000. Brazil's native population fell from 2.5 million to under a million within a century of the arrival of the Portuguese. The pattern was nearly the same throughout the Americas, where a total estimated population of some 50 million in 1500 was reduced to barely 8 million in 1600, before beginning a slow recovery. Although foreign diseases were the primary cause for such a disaster, the destruction of Indian communities, disruption of established patterns of agriculture, and forced labor on European mines and plantations also played deadly roles.

Still, in Spanish America, most food production, road construction, and mining were carried out by Native Americans. Because the mines in Mexico were located away from the major Indian populations, mine owners there soon relied on Indian workers brought in from elsewhere and paid (low) wages. In Peru, in contrast, a rotational system of forced labor was imposed on Indian communities and was only slowly supplemented by wage labor. After the Dominican friar Bartolomé de Las Casas campaigned against the mistreatment of Indians, royal authorities became alarmed that the greed and violence of the colonists would stimulate major resistance and revolt. Spain's "New Laws" of 1542 and after outlawed the enslavement of Amerindians and limited other forms of forced labor. At the same time, however, Spanish colonists began to purchase increasing numbers of African slaves, both because they were hardier and easier to manipulate than Native Americans and because the mineral wealth of Spanish America made their importation affordable.

Although various Meso- and South American peoples held slaves prior to 1492, Spanish conquerors first brought African slavery to the Americas in the armies of conquest that followed the early explorers. Cortés and his armies held several hundred slaves when they conquered Mexico in the 1520s; nearly 2,000 slaves were attached to the armies of Pizarro and Almargo that conquered Peru in the 1530s. Most of these black slaves were Spanish-speaking Catholics who had been born in Spain or Portugal of African forebears. In the fluid social environment of the conquest era, many of them gained their freedom or simply escaped. As colonial rule was consolidated over the next half century, African slavery became an important part of the South American economy, augmenting a much larger native peasant workforce, particularly in the cities of Mexico and Peru. Between 1521 and 1594, between 75,000 and 90,000 Africans were brought to Spanish-held territories, with over half going to Mexico. Nearly all of them were supplied by Portuguese shippers, who had a monopoly on the African trade under contract from the Spanish crown.

By the mid-1550s, Peru already was home to some 3,000 slaves, about half of them in the city of Lima. Then silver production developed at Potosí, making Peru and its capital Lima the wealthiest part of the New World. A major slave trade, funded by silver, arose mostly from Senegambia but also from West Central Africa. The long and arduous passage involved an Atlantic phase followed by transshipment to Pacific ports. Indian tribute laborers worked the silver mines in Peru under a system that the Spaniards adopted from the Inca Empire, while African slaves toiled in gold mining, urban industries, agriculture, cattle ranching, and diverse other occupations. In Lima, half the city's population was of African descent by1590.

As in Peru, slaves worked in Mexico in a variety of settings: in armies, farms, and in houses, especially in the urban centers, which Indians avoided. Initially Africans labored in silver mines, until they were replaced by less costly Indian wage workers. In 1570, roughly 50 percent of the population of Mexico City were African or descended from Africans. African slaves also produced sugar in and around Veracruz, where 40 or so plantations existed in 1600. But compared to Peru, Mexico's Indian population was much larger, African slavery was relatively less important, and the African-descended share of the population declined over time. Mexico's enslaved population peaked at some 35,000 by 1646—a large number, but less than 2 percent of the overall population. In contrast, at the same time, Peru contained close to 100,000 slaves, who constituted between 10 and 15 percent of the population. By the end of the 18th century, Peru had close to 90,000 slaves, while Mexico had only 6,000 left.

If silver provided the fortunes necessary for Spanish colonists to bring African slaves to the Americas, for the Portuguese in Brazil, it was sugarcane. By the first half of the 16th century, the Portuguese drew on their experience in Madeira and São Tomé to introduce sugar in Brazil. In northeastern Brazil, settlers created a major plantation system, producing for export to European markets. By 1575, Brazilian sugar planters were selling volumes of sugar that planters on the Atlantic islands could only dream about—as much as 130 tons a year per sugar mill, compared to 15 tons per year per mill in Madeira.

Initially the Brazilian plantation labor force was primarily composed of enslaved Indians captured in war or seized from their villages. Thousands of them died, however, in epidemics or from overwork or the harsh punishments meted out to those who resisted. The high death rate and rapid development of the sugar plantations created an insatiable demand for Indian slaves, prompting settlers from the southern region of São Paulo to organize slave raids deep into the interior to supply the plantations of northern Brazil. Northeastern planters also began to purchase slaves from Africa, who had some resistance to European-borne diseases and whose social alienation and distance from home made them easier to control than Native Americans. Sugar profits enabled planters to afford costly slaves,

delivered in growing numbers by the Portuguese shippers who dominated the Atlantic trade. By 1630, some 170,000 Africans had arrived in
Brazil and sugar was a predominantly black slave crop. Most of the
captives came from the Portuguese trading settlement at Angola,
founded in the late 1500s and centered around the port of Luanda.
This source of slaves proved so crucial to the development of northeastern Brazil that the Brazilian cleric António Vieira wrote in 1648,
"Without blacks there is no Pernambuco, and without Angola, there
are no blacks."

NORTHERN EUROPEANS AND THE EXPANSION OF THE SLAVE TRADE

Although African slaves labored in Spanish and Portuguese colonial
settlements from the early 1500s, it was not until a century later that
they were first brought to the territory that became the United States
of America. In 1619, twenty captives from Angola were landed at
Jamestown—not by English colonists, but by Dutch pirates who had
seized the Africans from a Portuguese vessel in the Atlantic. It was
the Dutch who first challenged the Portuguese monopoly on Atlantic
trade, granted initially in the 1494 Treaty of Tordesillas (by which the
papacy also divided South America between Spain and Portugal) and
reinforced when the Spanish and Portuguese crowns were unified in
1580. Moreover, by undertaking sugar production themselves and
later helping to spread it to newer English and French Caribbean
colonies, Dutch entrepreneurs expanded the slave trade and New
World slavery dramatically in the 17th century. Notwithstanding the
sale of African captives in North America at Jamestown, the British
and French Caribbean became the hub of American slavery and the
next frontier of the plantation complex.

The Portuguese held a virtual monopoly on the Atlantic slave
trade through its first century, in spite of other Europeans' occasional
forays to Africa. But Portuguese maritime commerce as well as
Brazil's profitable sugar industry attracted competition. In the 1600s
the Dutch launched a series of attacks on Portuguese overseas
commerce and colonization, partly as an offshoot of European
politics. Between the 1590s and the 1640s, the Dutch asserted their
political independence from the Spanish Empire, which at that
time also ruled Portugal. This put the Dutch into competition with

Portugal in Asia, Africa, and South America, as well as in Europe. The Dutch government chartered the East India Company in 1602 to compete with Portugal's Asian spice trade, and in 1621 the West India Company was created to seize Portugal's American and African possessions.[4] Following initial attacks on Spanish and Portuguese ships, a Dutch fleet in 1629 seized the Brazilian sugar province of Pernambuco, where Dutch planters and merchants took over and extended the sugar cultivation already there. The next step was to gain direct access to African slave supplies. Attacking first in West Africa, the Dutch seized Elmina in 1637 and eliminated Portuguese traders from the region. Then in the early 1640s, they temporarily took the Portuguese coastal base in Angola. The Dutch thus became a dominant European power in the Atlantic slave trading system, even holding the contract to supply slaves to Spain's colonies in the late 1600s.

Meanwhile, English and French colonists were beginning to set up farms and estates on Caribbean islands seized from or neglected by the Spaniards, hoping to profit from the cultivation and export of tobacco, indigo (a blue dye), cotton, and other crops. The English founded small settlements on Barbados and the Leeward Islands, while the French colonized Martinique and Guadeloupe. Unlike in Spanish South America, colonists from Europe found few Indians to exploit and had little access to precious metals to pay for imported slave labor. Instead, they staffed their operations through indentured servitude, an arrangement originally established in Virginia and then adapted in the West Indies. Over the course of the 17th century, between half and two-thirds of all white immigrants to the American colonies came as indentured servants. Some had been convicted of crimes and sentenced to penal servitude; others (including large numbers of children) had been abducted; while the majority voluntarily (though likely in desperation) exchanged several years' labor for the prospect of land, cash, and independence afterward. English merchants shipped some 200,000 indentured servants to the Americas in the 1600s, mostly to Virginia and Barbados; in the French colonies the numbers of *engagés* were much smaller—3,000–4,000 by

---

[4]For a full treatment of the Dutch East India Company (VOC), see Chapter 3 of the Connections Series book by Glenn Ames, *The Globe Encompassed: The Age of European Discovery, 1500–1700* (Pearson Prentice Hall, 2007).

the mid-1640s, comprising about half of the French population there. (See the first two sources at the end of this chapter.)

With indentured servants initially costing about half the price of African slaves, it was hardly inevitable that slavery would replace servitude in the English and French West Indies. But two developments propelled this shift: the establishment of sugar plantations, with major assistance from the Dutch, and the increasing difficulty of recruiting and managing European indentured servants. After Portugal retook its previously lost Brazilian territories in the 1650s, the Dutch began to profit not so much from their own colonies as from doing business with, and supporting, the colonies of Britain and France. Dutch shippers and traders brought slaves and sugar-milling equipment to the English and French Caribbean colonies, and later carried West Indian sugar to European markets. Dutch settlers, some of whom had cultivated sugar in Pernambuco, also established West Indian plantations themselves. These estates required large workforces who could be made to perform arduous tasks. But at around the same time, rising wages in England and competition from prosperous tobacco growers in Virginia meant that West Indian planters were finding it increasingly difficult to attract indentured servants. And the servants they did have organized rebellions against the cruel work regimes imposed on them. Under such circumstances, planters began to accept the costs of African slaves as necessary to ensure a stable workforce.

The tiny English colony of Barbados best illustrates the dramatic transformation that sugar brought to the 17th-century Caribbean. In the 1630s, Barbados's economy depended largely on tobacco, mostly grown by free and indentured European settlers. Its population totaled about 6,000, of whom 2,000 were indentured servants and 200 were African slaves. But slaves outnumbered Europeans (free and indentured combined) by the 1650s, and by the 1680s—by which time sugar had become the colony's principal crop—enslaved Africans were three times as numerous as Europeans. Exporting up to 15,000 tons of sugar a year, Barbados had become the wealthiest and most populous of England's American colonies. In fact, in 1700, Barbados was probably exporting more relative to its size and population than any other territory had up to that point in world history. With its large plantations combining both sugar growing and processing, based almost exclusively on African slave labor, Barbados provided a model that was later followed by planters in Jamaica, St. Domingue (Haiti), and elsewhere throughout the Americas. By 1700, the West Indies had

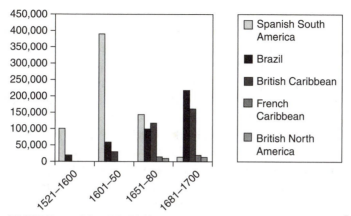

FIGURE 1.1   New World Slave Imports, by Destination, 1519–1700[5]

surpassed Brazil as the world's principal source of sugar and destination for slaves (see Figure 1.1).

Initially, most of the slaves were supplied by Dutch traders, now well established on the African coast. From the 1630s to the 1650s the Dutch West India trading company was the dominant European slave trader in Africa. It concentrated on the Gold Coast, particularly after the Portuguese retook Luanda and its other Central African port, Benguela, in late 1640s. But English, Danish, Swedish, French, and German companies organized similarly to the Dutch West India Company were not far behind, interested primarily in gold but also in buying slaves. These new companies established trading posts and made their own arrangements with African rulers, who often played different European nationalities against each other in order to maximize their own gains. French traders concentrated on the Senegambia region, where the Senegal Company established a trading fort at Gorée in 1671. The following year, in order to help ensure a continuous labor supply for its colonies, the French government offered to pay a bounty on each slave transported to Martinique or Guadeloupe; and by the end of the decade the French company had 21 ships operating in the trade.

---

[5]This chart and Figure 1.3 were created from data in the forthcoming second edition of the slave trade database, as presented in David Eltis and David Richardson (eds.), "Introduction," in *Extending the Frontiers: Essays on the New Transatlantic Slave Trade Database* (Yale University Press, forthcoming).

It was the British who came to dominate the Atlantic slave trade in its middle period, between the late 17th and early 19th centuries. Although individual English privateers had engaged in limited slave trading from the mid-16th century, there was little incentive until the expansion of the Barbadian sugar industry. English traders operated from the Gambia, Sierra Leone, and the Gold Coast, where an English fort was established in the 1630s, as well as part of West Central Africa. Like the Dutch and the French, the British government chartered a company with quasi-monopoly rights to its African trade. The purpose of the Royal African Company, established in 1672, was explicitly "to . . . set to sea such as many ships, pinnacles, and barks as shall be thought fitting . . . for the buying, selling, bartering and exchanging of, for or with any gold, silver, Negroes, slaves, goods, wares, and manufactures . . ." The Company's investors included the king and royal family, members of the English aristocracy, merchants, and even the philosopher John Locke. Coins minted in recognition of the enterprise soon were known as guineas, after the Guinea coast where gold was purchased, with a tiny elephant engraved below King Charles II's profile to symbolize the African trade. The Royal African Company established some 17 forts or stations on the West African coast, and between 1672 and 1689, its agents purchased nearly 90,000 African slaves for sale in the English colonies of the Americas.

THE 18TH-CENTURY PEAK OF THE SLAVE TRADE

Once plantation owners in the West Indies committed themselves to a labor force almost completely composed of African slaves, the numbers of captives torn from their homelands to toil in the Americas rose like the storm surge in a hurricane. There seemed to be no end to the European demand for sugar and other plantation products, consumed by a growing population with increasing purchasing power. In the Americas, a widening area of European control meant that ever more land could be turned into plantations. And their steady profits made it possible for planters and other employers to afford high-yielding investments in African slaves. In the 17th century, roughly 10,000 African captives were taken per year to the Americas; over the following century that yearly figure swelled to over 50,000. More than 80 percent of all slaves in the transatlantic trade were carried between 1700 and 1850, in spite of

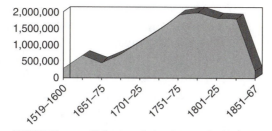

FIGURE 1.2 Volume of the Transatlantic Slave Trade over time[6]

the fact that this odious commerce had begun some two centuries earlier (see Figure 1.2).

As Figure 1.3 shows, the British and French West Indies, along with Brazil, drew the largest numbers of African slaves through the 18th century. Although the Atlantic slave trade had begun with imports to Spanish South America, those dropped significantly when colonists there could no longer afford to buy slaves at the high prices generated by booming sugar plantations in the non-Spanish Caribbean. Brazil, in contrast, consumed ever-rising numbers of African slaves, who worked not only in sugar production but also in gold mining and a range of other enterprises. Compared to the British and French West Indies and Brazil, British North America and the Spanish Caribbean were relatively insignificant destinations for African slaves.

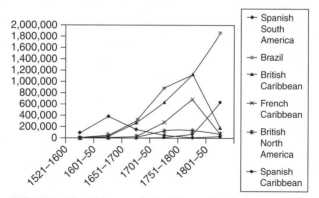

FIGURE 1.3 Volume of the Transatlantic Slave Trade over time, by Destination

[6]Derived from data in Table 2 of David Eltis, "The Transatlantic Slave Trade: A Reassessment Based on the Second Edition of the Transatlantic Slave Trade Database," unpublished paper.

The expansion of the sugar plantation system generated seemingly infinite demand for captive African labor in the British and French West Indies. During the 1600s, the meaning of the word *plantation* had changed from "a group of plants" to "an overseas settlement producing a tropical cash crop with unfree labor," and by extension to "an estate producing such crops, increasingly through the mobilization of black slaves." By the mid-18th century, the sugar plantation system occupied roughly 1.4 million slaves, or 40 percent of the 3.5 million African and African-descended slaves at the time; sugar production was by far the single largest slave occupation. By then the West Indian sugar industry was supplying the whole of the Western world, and it was so lucrative that plantation owners referred to sugar as "white gold." As a maimed slave says to a Frenchman in an illustration accompanying Voltaire's novel *Candide* (originally published in 1759), "It is at this price that you eat sugar in Europe" (see Figure 1.4).

While Europeans established plantations on islands throughout the Caribbean, the jewels in Britain's and France's American crowns were, respectively, Jamaica and St. Domingue (later renamed Haiti). Britain had seized Jamaica from Spain in 1655, and planters were quick to apply the lessons learned in Barbados to this much larger territory. By 1720, Jamaica had become the most populous slave colony in the British West Indies, and it soon produced more sugar than Barbados. Two decades later the island's 10,000 white colonists held 173,000 slaves, 75 percent of whom sweated and bled in the cane fields. The French colony of St. Domingue was chartered in 1664, and initially its settlers concentrated on producing indigo. But by the mid-18th century, St. Domingue had become France's premier sugar producing colony and also was becoming the world's largest producer of coffee. On the eve of the Haitian Revolution (which began in 1791), St. Domingue's slave population stood at 460,000, or nearly half of the 1 million slaves in all the Caribbean colonies.

In both Jamaica and St. Domingue, sugar plantations were larger than those elsewhere, employed greater concentrations of slaves, and worked them harder than ever before. While in Brazil and the other plantation societies of the 1600s, 50 or so enslaved laborers worked each plantation, the new plantations of the West Indies averaged about 200 acres and held about 100 slaves. These estates were integrated and often economically self-sufficient units, containing not only cane fields but sugar processing factories, as well as the kinds of artisan's workshops and food-producing plots necessary to sustain the whole enterprise. Part of the vicious efficiency of the sugar

C'eſt à ce prix que vous mangez du ſucre en Europe.

Candide Chapitre 19.

FIGURE 1.4 "It's at this price that you eat sugar in Europe," says a maimed slave to a French observer, in this illustration from Voltaire's *Candide*, originally published in 1759.

Source: Voltaire, *Candide ou l'optimisme: texte intégral*, Édition présentée, annotée et commentée par Jean Goldzink (Larousse, 1990), p. 132.

plantation was that the same set of slaves generally was put to work in multiple tasks—planting, tending, and harvesting cane; manufacturing sugar through tedious and dangerous factory work; as well as growing food crops, repairing buildings and roads, and tending animals. During the harvest season, when cane had to be processed quickly after cutting, men and women often worked 70–80 hours per week, continuing at night in the mill after toiling all day in the fields. (See the third source at the end of the chapter.) Pregnant women cut cane until shortly before they gave birth, returning to the gangs within a few weeks. The slaves were kept at work through intimidation and violence, ferociously punished for misdemeanors small and large. It is no wonder that in 19th-century Cuba, for example, it was said that *sugar is made with blood.*

The high mortality rates—due to malnutrition, disease, exhaustion, accidents, and physical abuse—coupled with a low slave birthrate and expanding demand for labor explain why the numbers of imported slaves kept rising. Slave reproduction was limited by female overwork and the fact that approximately twice as many males as females were imported from Africa. But with plantation profits high, planters calculated that it was more economical to work a slave to death and buy a replacement than to ensure the kinds of conditions that would allow the slave population to reproduce itself. Barbados's death rate was so astronomical, for example, that the importation of some 85,000 captives between 1708 and 1735 raised the total enslaved population from 42,000 to only 46,000. Jamaica and St. Domingue were worse still. Planters in Jamaica purchased a total of 750,000 slaves from Africa, but by the time of emancipation in 1838, the island's black population numbered just over 300,000. Between 1680 and 1776, about 800,000 Africans were brought to St. Domingue, yet the slave population numbered only 290,000 at the end of the 1770s. The first places where enslaved populations started to reproduce themselves were those with few or no sugar plantations: North America (except for Louisiana) from the mid-18th century, and Minas Gerais in 19th-century Brazil.

As these examples indicate, some slaves did other work besides feeding Europe's addiction to sugar. Although Brazil had been an early site for sugar production, employers in this enormous, diverse colony came to exploit slaves in a greater variety of enterprises than anywhere else in the Americas. In the late 1600s, a new gold and diamond mining industry in central and southern Brazil began to draw nearly as many African slaves as the relatively stagnant sugar industry of the northeast. Already by the 1730s the mining zones in the interior of central Brazil held over 100,000 African slaves; by the end of the 18th century, with flourishing diamond mines in and around Minas Gerais, the Brazilian mining industry held a quarter million slaves. It also gave rise to important urban centers like Rio de Janeiro (depicted in the fourth source at the end of this chapter), where slaves did both skilled and unskilled work in workshops, markets, households, and public institutions like hospitals and churches. To supply the miners of Minas Gerais, planters in the highlands around São Paulo produced foodstuffs on small farms, some with slaves. There and elsewhere, Brazilian slaves were also involved in cattle ranching, fishing, and maritime commerce. During the late 18th century, Brazil's northern provinces again saw economic expansion, this time with slave-grown cotton, and even later, coffee. Finally, as the Minas Gerais mining boom wound down in the early 19th century, slaves were deployed in production for the internal market. As of 1800, Brazil held close to 1 million slaves, making it the largest single concentration of African and Creole slaves in any one colony in the Americas at the time. (These days, 60 million Afro-Brazilians comprise the second largest African-descended population in the world, after Nigeria's.)

The territory that became the United States drew far fewer African forced immigrants than Brazil or the West Indies, with only 4 percent of total slave imports to the Americas. Indeed, at least three times as many migrants, free and enslaved, went to the English Caribbean than to the English colonial mainland between 1661 and 1710. With a climate unsuited to sugar cultivation (except in Louisiana), colonial North America saw a diversity of slave occupations similar to that in Brazil. In the early colonial period most slaves in the North farmed or were domestic workers; in the Chesapeake region they cultivated tobacco but also tended corn and raised livestock; in the low country of South Carolina and Georgia and in the lower Mississippi Valley they farmed, grazed livestock, and engaged in a variety of other activities. As in the rest of the Western Hemisphere, however, African slavery expanded dramatically in North America in the 18th century with the consolidation of major export industries. By the 1730s tobacco and rice production occupied about four out of ten North American slaves, while the majority was still employed in general farming, domestic service, crafts, or other nonagricultural work. But by the 1760s, about half of the mainland's slaves worked to produce three main staple crops: tobacco, rice, and indigo.

Although Africans were first brought to Jamestown in 1619, it was only around the 1680s that slaves overtook indentured servants as the major source of unfree labor in the Chesapeake region. Poor Englishmen (and small numbers of women) came to work in Virginia long after they had given up on Barbados because of the better availability of land and relatively more tolerable work regimes there. But a generation or two later, the same factors that limited the indentured population of Barbados—namely, rising wages in England and other employment possibilities for the destitute—prompted Chesapeake planters to turn to

African slaves as well. As the world's primary tobacco producers by the 1700s, Virginia's and Maryland's planters needed and could pay for imported laborers, who were supplied by the intensifying British slave trade. Chesapeake slave labor forces were generally smaller than those on Caribbean sugar plantations: tobacco estates tended to hold between 10 and 50 slaves, and many small planters had fewer. Still, the Chesapeake was early on the most important slave zone in continental North America, with 145,000 slaves by 1750.

At roughly the same time, 40,000 slaves lived and worked in the coastal low country of South Carolina and Georgia, mainly cultivating rice. South Carolina had been founded in the late 1600s by Barbadian planters who moved with their slaves in search of more land, bringing with them the practices and ideology of Caribbean slavery. They and others created a system of rice plantations much closer to the Caribbean model than to the tobacco enterprises of the Chesapeake. Rice became a viable export crop beginning around the turn of the 18th century, after its cultivation was perfected by slaves who faced food shortages and were encouraged to grow their own provisions. Initially, South Carolina's white settlers had been unable to grow rice because they understood little about how to do it. But their African slaves, torn largely from Senegambia and Sierra Leone, knew how to cultivate the crop because a variety of rice was grown in their homeland. By the end of the first decade of the 1700s Africans and their descendants comprised the majority of South Carolina's population, most of them toiling in the rice fields surrounding Charleston on plantations with 60–120 slaves each.

The third entry point for Africans into North America, initially a minor one, was Louisiana (French, then Spanish, then French again, then part of the United States as of 1803). Between the colony's founding and 1729, French ships landed just over 5,000 Africans there, two-thirds of them from Senegambia. But after that year, the French shut down their African slave trade to Louisiana in response to a massacre of the French settlement at Natchez, carried out by Indians with the support of African slaves, and a subsequent (suppressed) plot by Africans to kill all the Europeans and free themselves. As of 1740, the Louisiana slave population stood at 4,000, with most growing indigo and cotton; sugar was not cultivated in Louisiana until several generations later. By 1790, renewed slave imports (on British ships) combined with some natural increase brought the enslaved population to 18,700, a number that then nearly doubled over the next 20 years.

The plantation regime throughout the United States expanded dramatically after the turn of the 19th century, when Eli Whitney's cotton gin made cotton production more labor efficient and intensely profitable. Entrepreneurs gobbled up land beyond the frontiers of the coastal upper South, where they built numerous cotton plantations exploiting ever-greater numbers of African or African-descended slaves. Only one out of ten North American slaves worked on cotton plantations in 1800, but by 1860, the ratio was two out of three. The spectacular expansion of cotton farming in the southern states started just before the Atlantic slave trade was abolished in 1808, however, so the slave labor force primarily came from natural population growth as well as a massive internal slave trade. The same was true for Louisiana sugar, which planters began to perfect just about a decade before international slaving became illegal. Approximately 1 million enslaved individuals—women, men, and many children—were taken from the upper to the lower South in the 19th century, tragically separated from families and homes in the process.

Sugar production largely came to Louisiana with refugee planters fleeing the St. Domingue (Haitian) Revolution of the 1790s (which will be treated in Chapter 4). In Spanish Cuba, sugar production and African forced migration began a bit earlier, with some 65,000 slaves on the island by the 1780s. But Cuban exports soared after ex-slave revolutionaries virtually eliminated St. Domingue as a competitor on the world sugar market. By the mid-19th century Cuba was the world's primary cane producer as well as a major exporter of coffee, with roughly 50,000 Cuban slaves growing sugar and another 50,000 growing coffee in the 1830s. Slave ships continued to disgorge captured Africans at Cuban ports until 1867, when the Cuban slave population peaked at some 370,000.

SLAVERY AND RACISM

On Good Friday of 1622, Virginia's Powhatan Indians, threatened by the encroachment of English tobacco planters, staged a carefully planned attack on the Jamestown colony. By the middle of the day, over 350 colonists lay dead. On the Bennett estate alone, 52 were killed, and only five men were spared. Several years later, one of the survivors, Anthony Johnson, married a woman named Mary; over time they became the parents of four children. They farmed and raised livestock, and by the 1650s they owned 250 acres of land. In 1665, the family moved to Maryland's eastern shore, where they leased a 300-acre tract. Johnson's son John received a patent for 550 acres, and another son, Richard, owned a 100-acre farm. Johnson and his sons farmed independently, made use of the local courts, held slaves, and left their heirs sizable estates. So perhaps it might come as a surprise to know that in 1677 Anthony Johnson's grandson, John Johnson, named his own estate after his forebears' ancestral homeland—"Angola."

Anthony Johnson had arrived at the Jamestown colony in 1621 as "Antonio a Negro." He was probably a captive seized in the Portuguese wars in Angola, as were the first African captives who had arrived at Jamestown two years earlier. His wife, "Mary a Negro," also likely came from Angola sometime after his escape from Powhatan's warriors. Yet in the relatively fluid environment of early colonial Virginia, where most bonded workers were servants and not slaves, they eventually bought their freedom and acquired their own land. By 1650, Anthony and Mary were two of only 400 Africans in the colony, among nearly 19,000 white settlers. In the Johnsons' own county, at least 20 African men and women were free and 13 owned their own homes, although it was rare for any ex-servant—black or white—to own 250 acres of land.

Although the Johnsons were exceptional, their experience illustrates the comparative flexibility of race and slavery in the years before the plantation revolutions. Throughout the British and French American colonies, African slaves first worked in the fields side by side with white indentured servants or *engagés*. Whether they were black or white, bonded laborers suffered under brutal work regimes and living conditions, their movements were restricted, and they faced harsh punishments for running away. Marriage between Africans and Europeans was not uncommon (and interracial sex was more frequent still). Although they lacked indentured servants' specific promise of freedom, African slaves could sometimes become free through self-purchase or manumission. And colonial legal systems initially had little to say about slavery or race. In the French West Indies, King Louis XIV's *Code Noir*, issued in 1685, regulated slavery but was equally concerned with ensuring security, political subordination, and religious propriety in the colonies. It granted freed slaves the same rights and privileges as those enjoyed by the freeborn and made no social distinctions between free people of African and European descent.

But particularly in the English colonies (although later in the French West Indies too), laws and practices gradually separated white from black, even when their living and working conditions were similar. In 1636, the governor of Barbados announced that unlike Europeans, all Indian and African servants brought to the island would be treated as chattel slaves, as would their children, unless they had a contract of service specifying otherwise. The Master and Servant Act of Barbados in 1661 distinguished indentured servitude from outright slavery; the same year the Barbados Assembly drew up an "Act for the better ordering and governing of negroes." In 1662, Virginia lawmakers mandated that all children born in the colony to slave mothers would be enslaved, thus ensuring that slavery passed from generation to generation. And although laws tended to describe people designated for freedom (i.e., Europeans) as Christians, the Virginia Assembly ruled in 1667 that "the conferring of baptism does not alter the condition of the person as to his bondage or freedom." In the late 1660s, in efforts to further divide the laboring classes, Virginia and Maryland lawmakers provided new, harsher penalties for white servants who united with black slaves in running away, while farther south, the Fundamental Constitutions of the Carolinas stated that "Every Freeman of Carolina shall have absolute power and authority over Negro slaves of whatever opinion or Religion soever." In the 1660s, Virginia and Maryland banned interracial marriage, which eventually became illegal in all Southern colonies plus Massachusetts and Pennsylvania. After Anthony Johnson's death in Maryland in 1670, a jury decided that the land he left behind in Virginia could be seized by the government because he was a "negroe and by consequence an alien." African descent became a clear marker of slavery. In 1705, Virginia legislators mandated that "All servants imported and brought in this County . . . who were not Christians in their Native Country . . . shall be slaves. A Negro, mulatto and Indian slaves . . . shall be held to be real estate."

Although Old World slaves were generally considered to be outsiders, there was no prevailing notion that slaves would always be of a particular "race." Indeed, "race" as we commonly think of it didn't even exist before the plantation revolution: Europeans and others had many ways of defining and categorizing people, but this was generally on the basis of language, culture, religion, and geographic origin rather than on any assumed inherent, biological qualities. Recent research in human genetics has confirmed that "racial" differences are really only skin-deep: while human DNA does vary in some ways, skin color is no marker of other genetic categories, and genetic variations within geographically based groups (like Scandinavians or South Asians) are larger than those between such groups. Nevertheless, over the past several centuries, Europeans, Americans, Africans, and their progeny came to believe that all people of European descent shared certain inherent character-istics, as did all people of African descent; that the two groups were fundamentally different from one another; and that they could be distinguished on the basis of skin color and other physical markers. Moreover, according to the ideology of white supremacy that tragically lingers with us, people with European ancestry deserve to dominate people with African ancestry because they are inherently more capable. In the era of slavery many white people argued that black people were destined to be slaves because they were suited only for menial labor.

Racial ideologies undergirded the terror and coercion fundamental to keeping slaves at work. In every slave society, masters and overseers whipped, maimed, raped, humiliated, and deprived enslaved people—tortures they would have considered unthinkable for (most) fellow whites. They drove African-descended people like beasts of burden and inventoried them like cattle. They gave slaves names normally used for dogs, horses, or cows, like "Juno" and "Fido," or mocked them with grandiose appellations like "Caesar" and "Scipio." Yet even as the master class treated black people like members of an inferior species, they did not hesitate to exploit their human capacities for understanding and executing complex tasks—or for gratifying white people's sexual cravings, suckling their children, or caring for their intimate personal needs.

Scholars generally agree that virulent white supremacy developed as African slavery took root in the Americas, at slightly different times in different places. Yet historians interpret the precise relationship between racism and slavery in varying ways. Some argue that Western Europeans were already inclined to place Africans and Europeans in separate categories—one as outsiders subject to enslavement, and the other as insiders protected from such a fate. Partly, this was because of color symbolism: according to the *Oxford English Dictionary*, the meaning of "black" before the 16th century included, "Deeply stained with dirt; soiled, dirty foul.... Having dark or deadly purposes, malignant; pertaining to or involving death, deadly; baneful, disastrous, sinister. . . . Foul, iniquitous, atrocious, horrible, wicked." Even before American slavery was seriously underway, Western Europeans associated the color black with negative attributes like sin, sexual license, and devilishness, in contrast to the presumed virtuous color white. And when they encountered Africans, Englishmen and other Europeans identified their skin color as *black*, rather than any shade of brown, immediately drawing upon longstanding color connotations. Moreover, these associations had a religious inflection. Protestant and Catholic Europeans by the 16th century widely believed that African people were marred by the Biblical "curse of Ham" (Gen. 9: 18–27) that consigned them to lifelong servitude and which was manifested in their dark skin. Africans were not Christians (although some actually were, as in Kongo or, for a much longer time period, Ethiopia)—a primary means of identifying "insiders" for Western Europeans—and their dress, language, and habits seemed strange and even savage. Even if these cultural differences or color associations did not *cause* Europeans to take Africans as slaves, scholars of this viewpoint suggest, they certainly helped lay the ideological groundwork, allaying the qualms of Europeans who might otherwise have found slavery and the violence upon which it rested morally repugnant.

While acknowledging some of this cultural background, other scholars place much greater emphasis on economic factors in shaping African slavery. According to this point of view, African slaves became the preferred labor force for New World planters not because they were black or not Christians, but because of practical considerations, which became clear to planters through trial and error over time. First, because plantations required large numbers of workers performing back-breaking tasks, there was never any real possibility that American estates would be staffed entirely with wage earners—it simply would have cost too much to develop wage-labor plantations (although this puts aside the question of whether plantations themselves were inevitable or desirable).

On the other hand, unfree labor was theoretically available in European or African varieties. As discussed earlier, indentured servants and *engagés* did much of the work in the early British and French colonies. But estate owners and operators ultimately determined that African slaves were available in greater numbers than European servants and at lower costs, their productivity was higher, and they were easier to control. First, because of expanding economies in Europe beginning in the 1600s, the supply of new indentured servants could not keep pace with the rapacious demand for plantation workers. African suppliers, however, exported ever-greater numbers of captives (a process to be dealt with in Chapter 2). Moreover, slaves were essentially *stolen goods*—that is, they were kidnapped—and the prices charged for them therefore could be relatively low and still turn a tidy profit for their sellers. European indentured workers also toiled for finite periods of time, after which they were generally paid in land, goods, or money. In contrast, slaves did not have to be paid beyond the minimum required for their subsistence, and their labor was for their entire lives (tragically shortened as they were by disease and overwork). Finally, as easily identifiable outsiders, Africans were less likely to successfully rebel or escape, and somewhat easier to control, than European servants were. Once a sizeable slave population was already in place, identities began to be reworked—with a new and more intense emphasis on "race"—to justify and maintain the plantation system. Racial ideologies then began to live on their own, perpetuated by inequalities and shared even by non-slaveholding whites and people of African descent who claimed new identities in the Americas.

The alignment of African descent and slavery, and variations across different locations, can be seen in the small numbers of free people of color in the plantation societies of the Americas. In British North America the proportion of free people among the African-descended population peaked in 1790 at nearly 8 percent, declining after that. In the sugar-producing colonies of the West Indies, the proportions were even smaller. By the end of the 18th century, free people comprised 5 percent of the total population of color in the French West Indies, compared to 2.5 percent on the British islands. The mainland Spanish and Portuguese colonies offer a sharp contrast. In Brazil, free people made up about one-fourth of the African-descended population in the 1780s, while in Spanish South America, free people of color were 2.5 times as numerous as slaves. There are logical explanations for these discrepancies: Brazil's planters, historians have argued, created various distinctions and privileges among people of color as a way of dividing an enormous and potentially dangerous slave labor force; and African slavery had become relatively insignificant in Spanish South America, where a rebounding native population provided the vast majority of workers. But there were also national differences in racial ideologies and practices, with the English system the most rigid, followed by the French, and the Spanish and Portuguese more attentive to different shades and conditions of those of African descent. In all of the slave systems of the Americas, however, darker-skinned people worked for lighter-skinned people, and not the other way around.

CONCLUSION

In its firm association with a particular "race" and its enormous scale, slavery in the Americas differed from every other system of unfree labor that had preceded it. Yet it did not emerge onto the world scene out of nowhere. There had been masters and slaves for thousands of years prior to the first African importations to the Americas, and the Roman Empire was a *slave society*. When slavery largely disappeared from Western Europe in the Middle Ages, laws and customs governing it remained, to be drawn upon centuries later. Similarly, the slave-worked plantations of the New World had their precedents in the Old, with smaller-scale operations on the Mediterranean and Atlantic islands where planters worked out the techniques of sugar production and long-distance marketing. Even the new, virulent anti-African racism of the Americas had its antecedents in cultural prejudices of early modern Europeans.

But the plantations that were created in the Americas were new entities, built of European capital and management, American natural resources, and largely African labor, producing goods for sale halfway around the world. They were made possible when Europeans learned to navigate the Atlantic—a corridor for exchange as significant then as the Internet is now. In the relentless pursuit of profits, plantation owners demanded the lives of some 12 million Africans and their descendants. The vast majority of these tortured, overworked, and malnourished individuals toiled to create sugar, a mere luxury. And while their strength, expertise, and endurance literally built the new societies of the Americas, enslaved Africans and their descendants were denigrated as members of a sub-species of humans, unfit for freedom. The slave trade utterly transformed the world in ideological as well as material ways, and left a scar as deep as the Atlantic Ocean.

SOURCES

■ Masters, Servants, and Slaves in 17th-Century Barbados

The Englishman Richard Ligon lived in Barbados between 1647 and 1650. There, he observed the early stages of sugar production in the Caribbean. In 1657 he published a general account of the island, covering physical geography, plants and animals, and social and economic conditions. Ligon's account of the sugar industry suggested that great fortunes could be made for landowners in Barbados, yet he was grimly matter-of-fact about conditions for the island's separate classes.

What can you infer from Ligon's account about what brought immigrants to Barbados? How would you compare the conditions of indentured servants and slaves? How do you think they were prevented from rebelling? What kind of language does Ligon use to differentiate what we now think of as "racial" groups?

It were somewhat difficult, to give you an exact account of the number of persons upon the Island, there being such store of shipping that brings passengers daily to the place, but it has been conjectured . . . that there are not less than 50 thousand souls, besides *Negroes*, and some of them who began upon small fortunes, are now risen to very great and vast estates.

The Island is divided into three sorts of men, *viz.* Masters, Servants, and Slaves. The slaves and their posterity, being subject to their Masters forever, are kept and preserved with greater care than the Servants, who are theirs but for five years, according to the law of the Island. So that for the time, the servants have the worser lives, for they are put to very hard labor, ill lodging, and their diet very slight. . . .

As for the usage of the Servants, it is much as the Master is, merciful or cruel; those that are merciful, treat their servants well, both in their meat, drink, and lodging, and give them such work, as is not unfit for Christians to do. But if the Masters be cruel, the Servants have very wearisome and miserable lives. . . . I have seen an Overseer beat a Servant with a cane about the head, till the blood has followed, for a

---

Source: Richard Ligon, *A True and Exact History of the Island of Barbados* (London: Frank Cass, 1976) [orig. 1657], pp. 43–6.

fault that is not worth the speaking of, and yet he must have patience, or worse will follow. . . .

It has been accounted a strange thing, that the *Negroes,* being more than double the numbers of the Christians that are there, and they accounted a bloody people, . . . that they should not commit some horrid massacre upon the Christians, thereby to enfranchise themselves, and become masters of the Island. But there are three reasons that take away this wonder; the one is, they are not suffered to touch or handle any weapons; the other, that they are held in such awe and slavery, as they are fearful to appear in any daring act. . . . Besides these, . . . they are fetched from several parts of *Africa,* who speak several languages, and by that means, one of them understands not another.

■ The Population of 18th-Century St. Domingue

At the beginning of his encyclopedic *Description,* written before the massive slave uprising but first published in Philadelphia in 1796, the Martinican-born lawyer Moreau de Saint-Méry portrayed the different classes of people living in St. Domingue at the end of the 18th century. He drew on scientific theories of the era as well as his own observations and popular beliefs.

In his account, why did African slavery become so important to the French West Indian colonies? What traits does he attribute to the Africans in St. Domingue? What can you deduce about the values and views of the colony's white elite? And how did St. Domingue's 18th-century population differ from that of Barbados described in the previous document?

All the French Colonies in the Antilles had African slaves from the start. The Island of Santo Domingo already had them, since its first [Spanish] conquerors had possessed them at that time for nearly a century and a half. . . . It would be easy to believe that during the beginnings of the efforts of the Adventurers, they carried off some negroes . . . from their enemies and that it was only in devoting

---

Source: Médéric-Louis-Élie Moreau de Saint-Méry, *Description topographique, physique, civile, politique et historique de l'Isle française de l'Isle Saint-Domingue,* 1797. Translated, abridged, and edited by Ivor D. Spencer as *A Civilization That Perished: The Last Years of White Colonial Rule in Haiti* (Lanham, MD: University Press of America, 1985), pp. 39–42.

themselves to agriculture that they had a real need for Africans. They were to be seen for quite a long period cultivating with their own hands, in association with a sort of white slaves called "Engagés" or "Thirty-Six Months." These names expressed their servile state and its length.

Indentured service could not survive in the French islands, however. It was only until the time when tobacco was the chief and just about the only product of colonial trade, that the indentured servants were found suitable for the same employment as blacks. But the raising of indigo and especially of sugar cane implacably demanded men more capable of standing the continual effect of the hot sun. Also, this crop . . . offered ample earnings with which to pay for the negroes whom merchants were having sent from Africa. . . . The number of slaves kept on increasing. . . .

The indentured servants, who had continued to be transported—in small numbers—and whom the laws several times boldly directed the ship owners to bring over free of charge . . . became merely foremen to the gangs of blacks. . . .

The Africans transported to Saint-Domingue remain in general indolent and idle, quarrelsome and talkative, and liars, and are addicted to stealing. Always given to the most absurd superstitions, there is nothing which does not frighten them more or less. Incapable of analyzing religious ideas intellectually, they turn all their belief to external manifestations. If they go to church, they mumble some prayers which they have half learned, or indeed they fall asleep. . . .

◼ Sugar Production in Jamaica

As a young man, Zachary Macaulay (1768–1838) spent five years as assistant manager on a sugar plantation in Jamaica. After returning to England in 1789, he experienced a religious conversion and joined the British abolitionist movement. In the following excerpt, he recounts the experiences and observations of the Rev. Thomas

Source: Zachary Macaulay, *Negro Slavery; or, a View of Some of the More Prominent Features of That State of Society, as It Exists in the United States of America and in the Colonies of the West Indies, especially in Jamaica,* 1823. This excerpt was published in Graham W. Irwin, *Africans Abroad: A Documentary History of the Black Diaspora in Asia, Latin America, and the Caribbean during the Age of Slavery* (New York: Columbia University Press, 1977), pp. 206–8.

Cooper, who in 1817 was engaged by an absentee plantation owner to go to Jamaica and establish a plan for the religious instruction of the estate's slaves. A "man of great benevolence," this owner presumably kept his slaves under conditions no worse than those on the typical Jamaican plantation.

As you read this, consider the daily lives of the estate's slaves. Why wasn't Rev. Cooper able to find a time to preach to the slaves? What were their working hours during the harvest season?

One great obstacle to his success as a religious instructor, which Mr. Cooper had to encounter at the very outset of his undertaking, was this, that the slave had no time to attend upon him. This will require a somewhat lengthened explanation, which will serve, at the same time, to throw light incidentally on several material features of the slave system.

The season of crop, in other words, the sugar harvest, commenced about the time of Mr. Cooper's arrival in Jamaica, and continued for about five months. During that period, the general plan is, . . . to begin the manufacture of sugar on Sunday evening, and to continue it generally, without intermission, either day or night, till about midnight of the following Saturday, when the work stops for about eighteen or twenty hours, to commence again on the Sunday evening. In order to prevent any interruption of this process during the week, the slaves capable of labor, are, . . . divided into two gangs or spells, which, besides being both fully occupied in the various occupations of the plantation during the day, are engaged the whole of the night, on alternate nights, in the business of sugar making. Their labor, during crop time, is thus equal to six days and three nights in the week. And in the exaction of this labor, no distinction is made between men and women: both are subjected to the same unvarying rule. . . .

Sunday was *the only day which was allowed to the slaves, during crop, for cultivating and keeping in order their provision-grounds, from which provision-grounds they derived their sole means of subsistence,*[7] if we except a weekly allowance of seven or eight herrings to each adult, and half that number to each child, and a small present of a pound or two of salt fish at Christmas. If, therefore, they neglected to employ in their provision-grounds a sufficient portion of the Sunday, to secure them an adequate supply of food, they might be reduced to absolute want; and although the want might be supplied, yet the neglect would not fail to be punished.

---

[7]Emphasis in the original.

■ Urban Slavery in 19th-Century Brazil

Thomas Ewbank, an American traveler, resided in Rio de Janeiro for about six months in 1846. His account describes life in the city in detail, with particular emphasis on the customs of its population. As you read it, consider the following questions: What sort of work did slaves in Rio do? Where were they from? How important do they seem to be to the city's economy? How does this urban slavery compare to the rural slavery described for Jamaica in the previous document?

Slaves of both sexes cry [advertise] wares through every street. . . . Shoes, bonnets ready trimmed, fancy jewelry, toy-books for children, . . .—these things, and a thousand others, are hawked about daily.

When a customer calls, the slave brings his load, puts it down, and stands by till the owner delivers the articles wanted. . . .

Young Minas and Mozambiques are the most numerous, and are reputed to be the smartest *marchandes*.[8] Many a one has an infant added to her load: she secures it at her back by a wide piece of check [cloth] wound round her waist. . . .

I . . . continued on to the Campo—a spacious square, on the sides of which several national buildings stand, including the Senate-house. Covered with stunted grass, and the site of one of the principal fountains, it is the city's great washing and bleaching establishment, and is ever alive with lavandeiras [washerwomen]. More than two hundred are now scattered over the field, exclusive of crowds at the fount. . . . Some are Minas and Mozambique girls, as evinced by their superior forms, and attentions to attire. . . .

I emerged from the long avenue in Direita Street, not far from the Custom-house, where street-passengers have to run amuck through piles of bales, barrels, packages, crates, trucks, and bustling and sweating negroes. Here are no carts drawn by quadrupeds for transportation of merchandise. Slaves are the beasts of draught as well as of burden. The loads they drag, and they roads they drag them over, are enough to kill both mules and horses. . . .

Neither age nor sex is free from iron shackles. I met this morning a very handsome Mozambique girl with a double-pronged collar on; she could not have been over sixteen. . . .

Source: Thomas Ewbank, *Life in Brazil; or a Journal of a Visit to the Land of the Cocoa and the Palm,* 1856 (New York: Harper & Bros., 1856), pp. 92–149 and 113–18.
[8]Vendors.

With a friend I went to the Consulado, a department of the Customs having charge over exports. Gangs of slaves came in continually with coffee for shipment. Every bag is pierced and a sample withdrawn while on the carrier's head, to determine the quality and duty. . . .

Every gang of coffee-carriers had a leader, who commonly shakes a rattle, to the music of which his associates behind him chant. The load, weighing 160 lbs, rests on the head and shoulders, the body is inclined forward, and the pace is a trot or half run. Most are stout and athletic, but a few are so small and slightly-made that one wonders how they manage to keep up with the rest. The average life of a coffee-carrier does not exceed ten years. In that time the work ruptures and kills them. . . .

Why Did Africans Sell Slaves?

COMMON MYTHS

On a sunny afternoon in 1767, 17-year-old Kunta Kinte heads to the forest to find wood for a drum he will make as a present for his brother. He never returns home. Instead, he is chased through the woods to a clearing, where four armed men surround him. Urged on by a European with a gun, they trap Kunta Kinte in a net. In spite of his desperate attempts to defend himself and escape, Kunta Kinte ends up on a slave ship headed for Virginia.

Roughly 130 million Americans saw this depiction of the African side of the slave trade in the 1977 television miniseries *Roots*. Based on oral tradition, documentary research, and a good deal of imagination, the program—along with the book on which it was based—traced the struggles of author Alex Haley's family from the 18th-century Gambia to the 20th-century United

States.[1] Both the enormously popular series and the prize-winning book forcefully brought slavery and racism to the attention of the contemporary public. Yet the portrayal of the slave trade in *Roots* also reinforced some inaccurate understandings: as suggested in this book's Introduction, net-wielding white men did not creep onto African shores to nab would-be slaves as they engaged in their daily activities. Rather, Europeans nearly always *bought* slaves from coastal African sellers under arrangements of mutual agreement. How and why, then, did Africans sell slaves?

This question becomes even more puzzling when one considers the African effects of the trade, both on individual lives and on communities. The loss of millions of people adversely shaped Africa's demography, economies, and societies—not to mention the lives of the captives and their families. Yet how can we reconcile the harm done by the slave trade with the fact that Africans sold slaves voluntarily? And didn't anyone try to stop it?

GENERAL INTERPRETATIONS

When people realize that Africans *sold* slaves to Europeans, they tend to interpret this in one of two ways. One approach is to assume that African elites were controlled by European traders, who *forced* them to sell slaves. Or perhaps African leaders were simply immoral and greedy, selling out their own people for short-term gains. Both of these interpretations not only misrepresent the historical reality of the slave trade, but also give rise to unfair stereotypes about Africans. The first, that Africans were compelled to sell slaves, patronizingly presumes that African leaders were always weaker than Europeans. The second view, that African leaders brazenly sold their own people, imposes a modern identity category—"African"—on a past in which that category did not exist. Moreover, it tends to "blame the victim" by centering responsibility for the slave trade on "Africans" as a whole, rather than differentiating sellers and slaves, and rather than attributing responsibility both to African sellers and to European buyers.

The fallacy that Africans were overpowered by Europeans, who forced them to sell slaves, is belied by the obvious fact that Europeans

---

[1]Scholars of Senegambia and the United States have pointed to a wide range of historical inaccuracies in *Roots*, which even author Alex Haley admitted was comprised of both fact and fiction.

did not colonize and establish plantations in Africa (at least until the late 19th century, well after the Atlantic slave trade had been abolished). This is not because Europeans *chose* to leave Africans unconquered, but rather because, unlike in the Americas, Europeans had no significant technological or military advantage over Africans. Over the years, Europeans joined African military expeditions and individual Europeans served as mercenaries in African armies, but in Africa there were no equivalents to the conquistadors in the Americas. The only major war between Europeans and Africans during the slave trade era—in Angola beginning in 1579—rapidly became an indecisive standstill (as will be discussed below).

If Europeans could not conquer African societies, couldn't they at least stage individual raids and carry off slaves, like in *Roots*? Actually, it was difficult for ocean-going ships to approach the African coast, and they usually were met by African canoes well adapted to local waters. But occasionally European mariners did stage surprise raids. The English privateer John Hawkins led an expedition to kidnap African slaves in 1568, as recounted in the second source at the end of this chapter. At Cape Verde, his party was shot at with poisoned arrows; at the Gold Coast, he tried making an alliance to raid for slaves with an African king but was disappointed when the African warring party came away with more captives than his did. As mentioned in the Introduction, early Portuguese expeditions in Senegambia tried to capture slaves by force but soon were repelled. Even when slaving raids were successful, the retribution imposed on those who followed deterred others. One of the earliest North American voyages, made from Boston in 1645, was involved in raiding, and city officials actually returned the slaves seized by the ship, with an apologetic note, probably to retain or regain good relations with their potential trade partners. A century later, in 1747, the British government prohibited ship captains from unjustly seizing African people and imposed a stiff fine of £100 for offenders.

Africans' position of strength vis-à-vis Europeans in the early years means that they were not *forced* to sell slaves. In fact, there are portions of the West African coast where Africans never participated in the slave trade to any great extent. The region between modern-day northern Liberia and the eastern end of the Ivory Coast was fairly densely populated, and its inhabitants sold goods like ivory, pepper, wood, and cloth to visiting Europeans. But this was not a slave-trading area, and neither was most of what is now coastal Cameroon and Gabon, although people there exported other commodities. Thus the African leaders and merchants who entered the slave trade did so voluntarily, on their own terms. In every place except Portuguese-administered Angola—where Portuguese traders did exert some influence in the interior through cooperation with local rulers and with the assistance of local Luso-Africans, the offspring of Portuguese and African parents—European slave dealers acquired African slaves through peaceful trade that was regulated by African governments.

But how could African elites justify selling slaves voluntarily? Weren't they undermining their own communities, and destroying the lives of their own people? Were African slave dealers simply greedy sellouts? In order to understand African slave supplies, it is necessary to realize that outside the slave systems of the Americas, the term *African* had very little meaning before the 19th century. As the continent with the longest human history, Africa was and is home to the greatest population diversity in the world. People there spoke (and speak) thousands of languages, practiced varying religions, dressed and comported themselves in a range of ways, and were loyal to innumerable extended families, clans, towns, chieftaincies, and kingdoms. A king who sold war captives to a European trader likely had no more sense of affiliation with those enslaved individuals than the European did, or than the king and the European did with each other. Like Europeans and just about all other groups of people in world history, Africans considered slavery to be a legitimate institution for incorporating, domesticating, and exploiting outsiders. The main difference between Western Europeans and Africans during the period of the slave trade was simply that Europeans drew the boundaries of their "insider" group (i.e., those who should not be enslaved) more expansively than Africans did. Thus, African traders and leaders were not selling "their own people." This idea is based on racial categories that did not exist at the time. Refusing to put modern-day concepts of race onto early modern Africans allows us to feel sympathy for those who lost their lives, freedom, and dignity in the slave trade, even as we know that African elites sold slaves voluntarily.

THE SLAVE TRADE, WEALTH, AND POWER IN AFRICA

If Africans sold slaves to Europeans not because they were overpowered by Europeans or because they were immoral sellouts, then why *did* Africans sell slaves? First, they did so because they saw nothing wrong with it: slavery was an accepted institution, especially for dispensing with "outsiders." And as we have seen, slave sellers did not consider those they sold to be of common stock as themselves, particularly in the context of political fragmentation. In fact, most newly enslaved individuals were war captives who originated from outside the boundaries of where they were sold. Second, and given this, selling slaves gave leaders an initially low-cost way of strengthening themselves and their followers at the expense of their rivals.

For decades, historians have debated the extent to which slavery existed in Africa before the external slave trade. While we know that slavery spread and intensified over the period of the Atlantic trade, it is also evident that slavery and commerce in captives existed beforehand. This especially makes sense considering Africa's historically high land-to-people ratio. In this enormous continent where diseases spread in the moist heat and periodic drought brings famine, the most intense human struggles have been to build up populations. People were the key to wealth and security, because it was human labor that produced food and goods, carving civilization out of wilderness. Precolonial West African societies could be either stateless or highly stratified. Regardless, the fundamental social and political unit was the extended family, with affiliations established by descent and marriage. The oldest man of the founding family in a village or hamlet would generally be the leader, in consultation with other elders. The test of leadership, at all levels, was the individual's ability to distribute resources and adjudicate disputes fairly, make alliances for security and prosperity, and command respect. If no leader with such skills existed in the group, people moved away to seek other associations. A leader was only strong insofar as he had people loyal to him, while a wealthy person (who often was a political leader too) was one who could mobilize the labor to clear and farm land that was largely there for the taking. This emphasis on people as power and wealth had several important implications: an enduring value on fertility, broad acceptance of polygyny (when one man marries more than one woman), and institutions for recruiting labor power, such as patron–client relationships and slavery. Even if pre–slave trade African societies were not *slave societies,* the importance of "wealth in people" made slave ownership a widespread and fundamental feature of African life.

Yet slavery in, say, 17th-century West Africa was not the same as slavery in 19th-century Jamaica. If we imagine different kinds of slavery as a continuum, with outright chattel on one end and something more like marginal kinship on the other, New World slavery and African slavery would lean toward opposite sides. Although some slaves in Africa lived as the sort of dehumanized property American slaves were forced to be, in most African contexts the rules and conditions of slavery were different. In Africa the status of a slave might change over time, from a heavily exploited outsider to someone who knew the local language and customs and was more or less assimilated into the owner's lineage as a junior member. His or her children might even be free. Moreover, slaves in Africa were used in many more activities than in Europe or the Americas, performing administrative tasks or serving in the military, occasionally in positions of command, in addition to working as personal servants and agricultural laborers. Unlike in the initial slave populations in the Americas, a majority of slaves in Africa were women, valued for their reproductive as well as their productive labor.

Although there was a legal basis in Africa for selling slaves, most of those sold for export were not from an established slave class, but were newly enslaved captives taken in war or purchased from bandits. As in Europe or elsewhere, African rulers made war for a variety of political, economic, and personal reasons: to increase their territory, to avenge wrongs done to them by neighbors, to gain influence in a region, to control key resources or travel routes, or to secure power internally against rival members of the ruling elite. Africa's abundant land and human diversity created the conditions for especially frequent warfare. Political fragmentation was acute, so there were many states that could potentially fight against each other. In addition, when African states waged war, the object was not to capture land but people, either as incorporated vassals or as slaves. As historian John Thornton has argued, wars for slaves in Africa were functionally equivalent to wars land in Europe. They brought wealth and power to states and their leaders by providing the person-power to clear the bush, grow food, produce goods, trade, and reproduce new generations. Alternatively, captives taken in war could be sold, with the proceeds also used to strengthen the victorious state. This explains why there was already a large slave population in Africa at the time of its first European contacts, and why wars continued to generate slaves.

But if the slave trade, both northward across the Sahara and to Europeans at the coast, allowed African leaders to sell people who were already prisoners—meaning that in a strictly economic sense, captives cost very little to produce—it is not the case that slaves were exchanged for poor-quality goods or even worthless trinkets. African sellers gave up their captives only for payments that were locally valuable. Europeans had to select their trade goods carefully to suit the specific and frequently changing demands of Africans from various coastal areas. Often European traders paid for captives with guns and ammunition, which makes sense since the trade was a way for states and individuals to increase their own wealth and power. Cowry shells—brought from Asia and used as currency in West Africa—along with metals and manufactured goods also entered the African continent as captives left it. But by far the largest category of trade goods offered by Europeans and demanded by Africans was textiles. Weavers all over Africa already produced plenty of cloth, but the imports manufactured in Europe or brought to Africa from Asia held enormous appeal as exotic markers of fashionable luxury.

How, the reader may wonder, could imports of cloth be worth the sacrifice of human lives, especially when Africans already made their own? The answer has to do with the concept of "wealth in people." Aspiring "big men" (i.e., those with wealth and power) could recruit people to their households, fiefdoms, or kingdoms through a variety of ways, including marriage (to as many women as possible) and the production of children, conquest and/or enslavement, or slave purchase. Another way would be to offer resources and/or protection to people of lesser means, in exchange for their loyalty and (some of) their labor. This process might take place on a relatively small scale within villages—where chiefs sought followers—or on a larger scale, with kings commanding the loyalty of subordinate officeholders, who themselves exchanged resources for the allegiance and service of subordinates, and so on down the line. As a highly prized luxury, exotic cloth was distributed from the rich and powerful to their clients, cementing bonds of patronage. The same was true of alcoholic drinks and tobacco, which European and later Brazilian traders also exchanged for African slaves. Paradoxically, Africans sold people in order to get the imported goods that would allow them to recruit people into their societies. In doing so, they essentially traded outsiders for insiders.

THE FIRST TWO CENTURIES OF TRANSATLANTIC SLAVE EXPORTS FROM AFRICA

Because slavery already existed in Africa, the necessary institutions were available to support a large slave market, which Europeans as well as Africans could participate in. Those who held slaves and did not intend to use them immediately could sell them for other resources that would strengthen the kingdom or its leaders. Such choices were based on the specific circumstances of the moment, especially in the early years of the Atlantic slave trade. Rulers and their followers often entered and left the trade for reasons that made sense in a given time and place. For example, a 1455 account by explorer-trader Alvise da Mosto, who visited the Senegambian kingdom of Jolof, includes a description of slave uses in the domestic economy and the observation that most slaves were captured in civil wars and wars with neighboring countries. Many of these captives were integrated into the domestic economy, but the rest were sold into the trans-Saharan network in exchange for horses. Horses then could be used as cavalry, to help expand the kingdom.

The Atlantic trade was also related to state expansion in Benin. As recounted in the Introduction, Portuguese buyers began doing business with this kingdom in present-day Nigeria in the late 1400s, buying an array of goods including captives for resale at Elmina. During this period, Benin's armies were expanding the reach of the kingdom into neighboring territories, and some of the captives from these military expeditions were sold to the Portuguese in exchange for luxury goods that accrued to the king and his administration. But this situation did not persist. In the early 16th century, the *oba* first raised the price of slaves and then limited their sale. These actions were likely related to the end of the wars of expansion: without such military expeditions, there were not enough slave captives to sell and also to use at home. Instead of exporting slaves, Benin's rulers put them to work producing cloth and pepper domestically, some of which was sold, along with other items, abroad.

In the kingdom of Kongo also, elites desired European imports, but they had little of interest to sell to the Portuguese other than slaves. After Benin stopped exporting captives in 1516, West Central Africa south of the Congo River became the main source of labor for the São Tomé plantations, and later for export to the New World. Slavery already existed in Kongo, and elites were willing to divert some of their slave labor to the external market. As mentioned in the Introduction, Kongo's leaders entered into trading and diplomatic relationships with Europeans as part of their own power struggles. Rulers distributed exotic trade goods to their subordinates, who then did the same thing with their own followers, helping to strengthen the aristocracy by securing the loyalty of provincial elites and ordinary people. But Kongo's king Afonso I (r. 1506–1542/3) fairly soon began to experience the kinds of problems with the slave trade that African leaders would have for the next three centuries: as kings tried to sell captive outsiders for the collective strength and benefit of their own people (or at least for the power and glory of their own realms), their rivals endeavored to do the same. Over time, leaders and merchants competed with each other for shares of the trade, leaving ordinary individuals increasingly vulnerable to violence and enslavement. Elites became tied to the trade, so that to disengage from it would be to risk their own personal positions, the strength and reputation of their kingdoms, and the safety of their subjects.

In 1526, Afonso sent two letters of complaint to the king of Portugal (one of which is excerpted at the end of this chapter), explicitly hostile to the way the slave trade was affecting his country. "[E]very day the merchants carry away our people," he complained in October of that year, "sons of our soil and children of our nobles and vassals and our relatives" who were being kidnapped, secreted away, and stolen by "thieves and people of low condition" driven by the desire to have "your things." The thieves were "our people," who took their victims away at night and sold them to Portuguese merchants, without Afonso's own guards knowing about it. Portuguese traders were simply guilty of not asking enough questions about who was free and who was not. From then on, Afonso announced, no slaves would be sold without the oversight of his officials, and none would be exported without his knowledge and consent.

Afonso's complaints reflected the monarchy's diminishing ability to control slave exports—a problem that intensified as New World demand for slaves increased after about 1530. As Kongo expanded through military conquest, its armies took captives from beyond the kingdom's existing borders, enabling the king to reward old and new provincial leaders with imported goods. But if the external slave trade helped strengthen the king's power initially, over time it had the opposite effect. Provincial heads and lineages were called upon to raise Kongo's army, but when they gained loot and slaves as spoils of war, they were in a position to challenge the king and even to engage directly with Portuguese traders. Moreover, there were practical difficulties with procuring slaves from the kingdom's frontiers: up to 50 percent of slaves died getting to the coast, while victimized populations organized themselves for defense.

Over the years, Kongo's leaders supplemented foreign captives with slaves from inside the kingdom, generated through domestic tribute and judicial trials. Amid growing discontent within the kingdom, rule by sheer force partially replaced the old links of patronage holding the system together. By the 1560s, there were rumors of mutinies, and two Kongo kings died successively in battles. In 1568 foreign warriors known as the *Jaga* invaded, joined by Kongo peasants in open revolt against their lords. The court fled to an island in the Congo River, from where the king appealed for Portuguese help. A Portuguese army arrived, which after seven years of war managed to re-establish royal authority. But after these events the king became ever more dependent on the export of captives in exchange for Portuguese support. During the 17th century, the Kongo kingdom disintegrated into rival regional factions, each fighting one another in pursuit of war captives. Provincial leaders dealt directly with slave traders to get guns and goods which they used to challenge rivals. While elites fought and intrigued for political power, ordinary people suffered a breakdown of civil order and constant threats (Figure 2.1).

With their ever-increasing demand for slaves, Portuguese traders benefited from the chaos in Kongo and also sought new sources of captives. In 1575, they established a slaving station at the Central African port of Luanda, from which they purchased captives from the *ngola* (king) of Ndongo, Kongo's southern rival. Within a year, the Portuguese started a war against Ndongo in hopes of conquering lands where silver mines were rumored to abound, and also to assert authority over slave trading there. Instead of silver, the Portuguese encountered stiff African resistance and tropical diseases. As the invasion burnt out in the late 1580s, the remains of the Portuguese army settled into the role of regular slave traders, based along the West Central African coast and into the interior. In 1591, the beginnings of the crown colony of Angola were established, administered from Luanda.

Around 1614, a Portuguese alliance with African mercenary groups called *Imbangala* broke the military stalemate. Rather than an

FIGURE 2.1   The King of Kongo receives Portuguese visitors, late 16th century

Source: Pieter van der Aa, La Galeríe Agréable du Monde (Leide, 1729), p. 51.B. (Library of Congress, Prints and Photographs Division, LC-USZ62-30839).

ethnic group, the Imbangala were independent gangs of soldiers and raiders who lived entirely by pillage. From diverse origins, they formed new political groups, or rather camps, called *kilombos* (similar to institutions which surfaced among escaped slaves in Brazil, as will be discussed in Chapter 3). With their Imbangala allies, Portuguese authorities were able to administer the Angola colony, from which they traded for slaves and destabilized nearby polities. (In fact, wars between the Portuguese with their Imbangala proxies and the Ndongo kingdom likely generated the captives who became the first Africans at Jamestown, mentioned in Chapter 1.) Portuguese traders acquired captives in two ways: by enacting treaties with African kings or subordinate chiefs that required them to deliver a set number of slaves in return for imports and good relations; or by sponsoring local warlords, some of whom were Portuguese or of mixed Afro-Portuguese descent, to raid for captives directly. Between the first

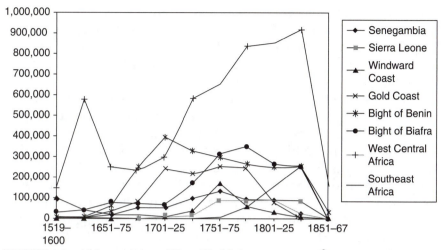

FIGURE 2.2   African origins of New World slaves, over time[2]

African slave arrivals in the New World in 1519 and about 1650, some 90 percent of the captives forced to cross the Atlantic came from West Central Africa, as Figure 2.2 shows.

EXPANSION OF THE TRADE

If the slave trade in the 16th and 17th centuries brought storm clouds to West Central Africa and elsewhere, by the 1700s it was as if tornadoes were engulfing much of Africa's western half. With American demand for slaves whipping up prices paid for captives on both sides of the Atlantic, Europeans and Africans were drawn into the vortex. On the buyers' side, hundreds of individual traders from England, France, the Netherlands, and Portugal competed with the chartered companies operating in West Africa. In Africa, as Figure 2.2 indicates, regions that had not supplied many slaves previously, such as the Gold Coast and the Bight of Benin, now became significant sending areas. In regions already involved in the human commerce, its scale swelled as large and small states as well as freelance merchants found the profits too compelling to ignore. West Central Africa continued to

[2]Tabulated from data in Table 5 of David Eltis, "The Transatlantic Slave Trade: A Reassessment Based on the Second Edition of the Transatlantic Slave Trade Database," unpublished paper.

provide the vast majority of captives, from a slaving frontier that moved steadily inland. But significant numbers also came from Upper and Lower Guinea, and by the end of the 18th century slavers were even rounding the southern tip of Africa to procure captives from the southeastern coast (which will be discussed in Chapter 4).

Even while the numbers of captives exported to the Americas rose horrifically, the same basic processes as in an earlier era produced slaves. As wars continued to be fought for more or less conventional reasons, selling captives weakened rivals and helped to finance the costs of war. The slave trade did not so much generate new wars as prompt more interest in selling captives, sometimes in exchange for munitions, rather than keeping them. And although Europeans did not really foster African wars by arming one power against another, they did benefit from the fact that both the purchase of guns and the sale of slaves were useful for African rulers in the course of seeking other political or economic outcomes. But if African leaders did not have to be persuaded to make war and sell captives, the slave trade also contained a dynamic beyond their control: even if they wanted to avoid trading in slaves, to do so would make those leaders, and their followers, vulnerable to the power of slave-trading rivals. For instance, Queen Njinga, who ruled Ndongo and its successor state Matamba from 1624 to 1663, is remembered today for her staunch resistance against Portuguese expansion. But she willingly engaged in the slave trade, at least in part to get the wealth and munitions necessary to wage near-continuous warfare.

In West Central Africa, two different, extensive networks for trading slaves had emerged by the later 17th century (Map 2.1). North of Luanda, in the area including the fragmented Kongo kingdom, the Portuguese lost control of the slave trade to Dutch, French, and English merchants, who carried Kikongo language-group speakers to the plantations of the Caribbean. In the southern network, Portuguese and Afro-Portuguese traders channeled Ovimbundu language-group speakers and others from the ports of Luanda and later Benguela in Angola primarily to Brazil. Each network was anchored by the coastal slave markets, connected by road to trading centers far inland where sizeable numbers of slaves could be bought. All along the road, caravans bought foodstuffs, local products, and some enslaved people, while selling European or African commodities. At the end of the trading routes lay the slaving frontiers, regions of turmoil in which

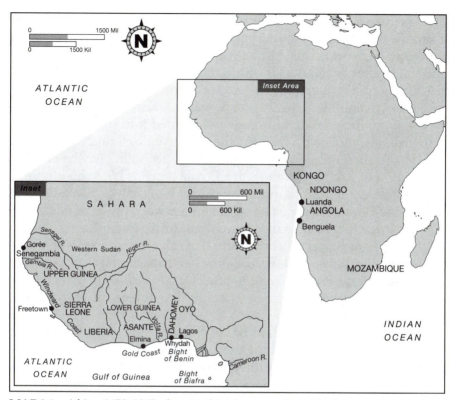

MAP 2.1   Africa, 1450–1865, showing locations mentioned in the text

chaotic kidnapping and war were the major sources of procurement. Some local populations reacted by fleeing away from such areas, others turned to raiding and piracy on the rivers, while others migrated toward markets that collected slaves in the hope of profiting from the trade.

One collective movement aimed at least in part at stopping the violence that fed the Atlantic trade was led by a young Kongo woman in the early 18th century. Kongo at this time was engaged in civil war, as it had been from the mid-1600s. Rival candidates for the throne had divided the country, established headquarters in mountainous regions and fought one another, generating captives for European traders, while Imbangala raiders threatened those at the fringes of the kingdom. The breakdown of order and discipline meant hunger for the common people—for farming was disrupted—as well as the loss of houses and possessions, and vulnerability to capture as slaves. In

1704, a 20-year-old Catholic noblewoman and spirit medium named Dona Beatriz Kimpa Vita declared that she was possessed by Saint Anthony. Following his instructions, Dona Beatriz traveled to the capital, where she rebuked the Kongo king for lacking the will to unify the kingdom. From all parts of the kingdom people came to hear her message, mainly that Jesus—who was of Kongolese origin—was angry about the warfare in Kongo and wanted it to stop. For the next two years, Dona Beatriz traveled the country promoting a new set of prayers, healing the sick, curing infertility, and calling for the political unification of Kongo and the end of enslavement. With thousands of her followers, she reoccupied the ancient capital of São Salvador, which had been abandoned in 1678. Her activities presented a powerful challenge to political and church authorities, who accused Doña Beatriz of heresy and witchcraft. In 1706, she was apprehended and burned at the stake. At least 5,000 of her supporters were captured and enslaved right away, with another 2,000 or so shortly thereafter. Thousands more were taken as prisoners in subsequent years of continued civil war. Some were sent to the southern slaving network and ultimately, if they survived, to Brazil. Others were taken through the northern network to English, Dutch, and French ships. Many ended up in South Carolina, where they may have been among the Central African Catholics who participated in the Stono Rebellion in 1739, attempting to escape South Carolina and seek refuge in Spanish-controlled (and officially Catholic) Florida.

Resistance to the slave trade may have slowed the pace, but Central Africa continued to produce many thousands of unfortunate captives. In the 18th century, the Kongo and Angolan coasts sent 2.4 million slaves into the Atlantic trade, with another 1.9 million following in the 19th century. The region represented nearly 45 percent of the total number of Africans shipped in the entire Atlantic slave trade. Captives from West Central Africa accounted for some three-quarters of the Africans imported into Brazil, as well as the majority of those brought to St. Domingue (Haiti) and Spanish-speaking South America. They came from a steadily expanding slaving frontier, which reached beyond demographically depleted or defensively organized populations.

After West Central Africa, the African region sending the next largest number of enslaved people to the New World was the Bight of Benin, or present-day southwestern Nigeria, Benin, and Togo. Around 60 percent of the captives from there were taken to Bahia, in northeastern Brazil, while another 20 percent or so of them were transported to the French West Indies. This region witnessed an enormous increase in slave exports in the second half of the 17th century, largely because of the development and expansion of two major trading states, Oyo and Dahomey, along with the smaller state of Whydah. In fact, between 1676 and 1725, the Bight of Benin—aptly known by Europeans as the "slave coast"—supplied more slaves to the Atlantic system than did any other African region. It did so with no significant European presence: foreign traders built no forts as in the Gold Coast or Senegambia; few European personnel resided there; and all trading occurred at the discretion of local authorities. "Beware, beware the Bight of Benin," said Europeans wary of tropical diseases, "for few come out though many go in"—although strong African states probably limited the European presence as much as microbes did. In exchange for captive people, African traders and rulers mainly imported Indian-made cloth and cowry shells, a currency in wide use in the Bight of Benin but rare elsewhere.

The drastic increase in slave supplies from the Bight of Benin seems to be correlated with the emergence of Whydah, a tiny kingdom in the present-day Republic of Benin. In the early 18th century, most slave traders doing business in the region stopped at Whydah, whose king even sent a delegation to the French court to ensure trade. But its vigorous foreign relations did not protect this microstate from conquest: Whydah was loosely subject to the larger kingdom of Alladah, and both were absorbed by Dahomey in the 18th century. Dahomey then became a major participant in the Atlantic slave trade.

Historians know about Dahomey from several sources, but perhaps the most curious of them center on one of the king's slaves, an Englishman by the name of Bulfinch Lambe (who features in the third source at the end of this chapter). His story begins in Alladah, where the British Royal African Company sent him in 1722 to arrange some business with King Sozo. The king, attempting to force the Company to settle a previous debt, detained Lambe as a hostage. Two years later, with Lambe still stuck there, the army of Dahomey laid siege to Alladah, intending to break into the coastal trade. Lambe was captured along with 8,000 others; while 6,000 of the prisoners were sent to Europeans at the coast, Lambe and the rest were brought inland. At the Dahomey capital, Abomey, Bulfinch Lambe became the slave of King Agaja.

As the first literate observer ever to visit Abomey, Lambe had a rare opportunity to observe life in King Agaja's capital firsthand. Through an interpreter, the king and Lambe held many long conversations. King

Agaja told Lambe that he had militarized the kingdom of Dahomey, establishing the best-trained and best-equipped army in the region. Soldiers carried flintlock muskets instead of the traditional longbows, as well as steel swords and cutlasses for close fighting—all imported from Europe—and locally made shields. King Agaja also acquired 25 cannons, although he confided to Lambe that he did not possess the formula for making his own gunpowder. While King Agaja was investing in his military, he was also establishing a royal monopoly on the spoils of war. Although soldiers received bonuses of cowry shells for each enemy killed or captured in battle, all prisoners taken by the army belonged to the king. Captives were used in a variety of ways: as religious sacrifices, as workers on the king's farms, as servants in the royal palaces, as patronage to army officers and royal officials, and as payments to European traders for arms, ammunition, lavish cloth, and cowry shells.

In the 1720s, Dahomey conquered Whydah and thereby gained access to the coast for trade. But within a decade, Dahomey was forced into a tributary relationship with Oyo (a kingdom in present-day Nigeria described below). After that, the Dahomean state less often used its military power to capture slaves and instead occupied a middleman position between northern suppliers and European merchants on the coast. The royal trading monopoly became theoretical only, as the state regulated commerce carried out by private traders. As merchants became rich, government revenue also largely became dependent on the slave trade, together with taxes on individuals and their activities and tribute in labor and foodstuffs from conquered areas. And the king remained the largest single slave trader in Dahomey. Thus, participation in the slave trade drew Dahomey into an international commercial network from which it could withdraw only at the cost of the possible destruction of its social and political system.

The other major source of slaves from the Bight of Benin, particularly as the 18th century drew to a close, was the kingdom of Oyo. Founded in the 14th century on the savanna woodland north of the tropical forest, Oyo was one of several city-states whose inhabitants spoke a variant of the Yoruba language and practiced roughly the same religion. In the 17th century, Oyo perfected its cavalry and began military expansion to the south (where tsetse flies make it impossible for local people to keep horses). Thirteen other kingdoms were annexed and became provinces of the Oyo Empire. Until its conquest of Dahomey in 1730 (through the so-called "Dahomey gap," a break in the forest which horses could penetrate), Oyo had only indirect commercial contact with the coast. Even after 1730, Oyo's most important trade was to the north, with suppliers of horses and slaves.

The power and wealth of Oyo's kings grew enormously during the 18th century. War captives or slaves purchased from farther north labored on royal farms, while tribute poured in from subject towns and villages, as well as Oyo's neighbors, and traders paid taxes on their transactions. The kingdom's incessant wars of expansion produced more captives than were needed on the royal farms. In return for "surplus" slaves sold to Europeans at the coast, Oyo's leaders received firearms, cloth, metal goods, and cowry shells, some of which were kept within the empire while some were traded to the Hausa states farther north for horses and more captives. Over the mid-1700s, Oyo became a major transit handler of captives from north to south.

The problem of controlling this empire destabilized Oyo, however. By the 1780s, subject provinces began to break away. In 1817, a dissident chief incited a revolt by Oyo's numerous Muslims which ended with the overrunning of the capital. By 1835 the capital at Old Oyo was deserted, and civil wars continued to fuel Yoruba participation in the slave trade. In the early 19th century the slave trade drew more heavily on Yoruba than on any other nationality, though Yoruba slaves had been practically unheard of in the Americas before 1750. Yoruba slaves left their cultural and material mark especially in Cuba and northeastern Brazil, where some people still speak Yoruba words and attend to Yoruba gods like Shango, Ogun, and Osun.

In Dahomey and Oyo, the slave trade became a major feature of economic and political life. But these states also had diversified economies, and it would be a mistake to attribute their development entirely to the slave trade. While the wars these states waged did lead to the capture and enslavement of thousands of unfortunate individuals, it would be difficult to prove that they fought solely to feed the Atlantic trade. Similarly, wars for reasons other than generating captives also fed the slave trade from the Gold Coast, where the Asante state began its rise to prominence around 1700.

At the beginning of the 18th century, Asante was a loose military alliance of several small states in the interior, which used guns and armies funded by the gold trade to consolidate and expand. The captives taken in these wars were used internally for agriculture and gold mining, particularly since Asante's trade with the coast was blocked by other states. Over the first two decades of the 18th century the Asante army conquered these states, giving Asante traders access to the coastal forts on a regular basis. They sold little gold, which was in demand within Asante itself, providing mostly ivory and slaves instead. These slaves may have been offered because Asante's rulers considered them to be "surplus," or they may have been sold because gold output from the mines was declining, and slave sales allowed elites to continue purchasing the types of imports previously paid for with gold. From about the 1720s, increasing numbers of slaves were taken from the Gold Coast, primarily by English and French buyers who traded guns and gunpowder as well as textiles used as luxuries.

Farther east, the Bight of Biafra was the third largest supplying region in the peak years of the slave trade, principally doing business with English merchants. In this mostly Igbo-speaking area of contemporary southeastern Nigeria, there was practically no European land-based presence. And uniquely in Africa, most captives from this region were not prisoners of war, but instead were kidnapped. The Niger Delta area was and is densely populated, with some very large settlements and easy river navigation from place to place. But there were no states to speak of, and government took place through village, lineage, and religious organizations. This extreme political fragmentation meant that everyone was more or less an outsider to people living not very far away, and no one entity was powerful enough to offer widespread security. Outlaws and bandits, lurking in the woods and highly mobile in watercraft, could strike and kidnap people practically at will. Olaudah Equiano, whose memoir was mentioned in Chapter 1 (and who composed one of the sources at the end of Chapter 4), wrote that as a child he was seized from a village in the Bight of Biafra through just such a process.

Far fewer captives were exported from Senegambia and the nearby Windward Coast and Sierra Leone. The mainly French and British traders who operated there bought commodities like gold and gum, as well as slaves captured through warfare and raiding. But even these regions saw a sharp increase in slave exports in the 18th century. The higher numbers can be attributed to rising European demand and high prices, in conjunction with two internal developments: the militarization of states in the Western Sudan (the hinterland of Senegambia) like the Bambara state of Segu and its rival Kaarta, beginning around 1700; and a series of Islamic revolutions, accompanied by warfare, closer to the coast. These changes indirectly contributed to both rice cultivation in South Carolina—perfected by Senegambian and Sierra Leonian slaves—and the 1729 and 1731 conspiracies in Louisiana, undertaken in large measure by Bambara slaves from the Western Sudan.

The Sierra Leone and Windward Coast ports, where British, French, and Portuguese traders established forts, were primarily conduits for slaves from Senegambia and the Western Sudan. But except for briefly in the 18th century, these three areas together (collectively referred to as Upper Guinea) never matched the volume of slaves leaving any other single slave-exporting African region, and for most periods they were only minor suppliers of captives to the Americas. This may seem surprising, since Senegambia, Sierra Leone, and the Windward Coast are the African regions geographically closest to the Western Hemisphere—in fact, directly on the water routes to and from other slave trading areas—and large portions of their populations lived within easy reach of the Senegal or Gambia Rivers. But several factors seem to have limited slave sales from Upper Guinea. First, for local reasons, the products Europeans offered in exchange for slaves were largely unappealing. Second, Islamic identity allowed relatively large numbers of people to be considered as "insiders" and not subject to enslavement. This, combined with the trans-Saharan and internal demand for slaves, meant that European merchants competed for relatively small numbers of captives. Finally, local people resisted. According to the slave trade database, Upper Guinea accounted for 13 percent of slave departures from Africa but 25 percent of shipboard rebellions. Nearly 60 percent of all attacks on slave ships by shore-based Africans took place off Senegambia and the Windward Coast, and there were bloody revolts at the coastal forts before ships even left port. Although the lure of the Atlantic trade was difficult for rulers and merchants to resist, the patterns from Upper Guinea show that common people were sometimes able to limit this odious commerce.

Finally, southeast Africa and particularly Mozambique supplied a small fraction of transatlantic slaves, mainly toward the chronological end of the trade. Mozambique's slave trade began during the Dutch occupation of Luanda (1641–48), when the Portuguese sought captives on the east coast of Central Africa. During the second half of the 18th century, French slavers populating their Indian Ocean island colonies (Mauritius and Réunion) bought captives in southeast Africa, later bringing some of them to St. Domingue. After the Haitian Revolution began in 1791, the transatlantic slave trade from Mozambique became primarily a Brazilian/Portuguese operation, intensifying after the British outlawed the transatlantic slave trade north of the equator in 1808. But the major east African slave trade, closely connected to the export of ivory as well, flowed to plantations on the Kenya coast and on the islands of Zanzibar and Pemba, as well as to Madagasgar and across the Indian Ocean through Islamic trading systems. As in the western part of Central Africa, captives were generated in Mozambique through unrelenting warfare and banditry, which brought political destabilization and human misery.

EFFECTS OF THE SLAVE TRADE ON AFRICA

Given the terrible poverty afflicting most Africans today, the question of how the slave trade affected Africa is of more than theoretical importance. In his influential book *How Europe Underdeveloped Africa* (1972) the Guyanese scholar-activist Walter Rodney argued that the slave trade and then colonialism were what impoverished Africa, to Europe and America's benefit. But while Rodney and his supporters have seen the slave trade as very influential for African history, other scholars believe they have overstated their case. These historians stress the relative marginality of the slave trade to Africa's overall history, as well as Africa's resilience in the face of it. They don't want to defend or minimize the trade, but they argue that African history has been shaped more by internal developments than external ones. In this attempt to understand the slave trade's impact on Africa, scholars have looked at demography, economics, politics, and social developments, among many factors, of which only a few can be surveyed here.

The trade's demographic impact is potentially the most important because the struggle to build up population has been so central to African history. It is difficult to be specific about the demographic ramifications of the slave trade, however, because precise population figures for precolonial Africa do not exist. Using an extensive computer simulation, historian Patrick Manning has made a demographic model that at least suggests some tentative conclusions. Based on 1931 census data and an assumed moderate population growth rate of 0.5 percent per year, Manning concluded that the area of western Africa supplying the Atlantic slave trade contained some 25 million people in 1700. Using the known statistics for the slave trade along with estimates of casualties, he calculated that the equivalent population had fallen to about 20 million by 1850, with the worst losses in Angola and the Bight of Benin. He also argued, though, that the true demographic cost must also include the likely population growth if there had been no slave trade. He reckoned that in 1850, if not for the slave trade, the population of all of sub-Saharan

Africa might have been about 100 million but was in fact about 50 million. This loss took place during rapid population growth elsewhere, so that Africa's proportion of the combined population of Europe, Africa, the Middle East, and the New World declined between 1600 and 1900 from about 30 percent to a little over 10 percent.

On the other hand, in the regions of heavy population losses, people probably adapted marriage and child-rearing patterns to help compensate. For instance, approximately two African men were deported to the Americas for every one African woman, leaving a "surplus" of women in slave-raided areas. In such situations, men married at younger ages than before, and polygyny expanded. Women took on the agricultural work previously done by men, while also caring for large numbers of children. This meant falling productivity at the same time as much harder lives for women, but it may have helped promote demographic recovery.

Population figures must also be considered in the context of new diseases that Europeans brought to Africa, and also of new crops that were introduced, like maize (corn) and cassava, which produce more calories per area of land than indigenous crops. The new crops almost certainly made more food available in a region of relatively poor nutrition, although cassava often provides fairly empty calories. New crops are a major reason for thinking that the potential for population recovery during the slave trade was high. On the other hand, the slave trade introduced new diseases like smallpox, tuberculosis, pneumonia, plague, and syphilis, although without the devastating effects they brought to the Americas. Overall, scholars do not know how severely the slave trade affected western Africa's demographic history. But there is no doubt that the estimated 4.3 million slave and free people of African descent living in the Americas in the 1790s would have made a significant contribution to the growth of African populations, and African economies, had they remained in Africa.

Aside from the economic losses resulting from population decline—like reduced agricultural activities, the abandonment of land, and widespread labor shortages—did the slave trade also impoverish Africa by retarding manufacturing? Some scholars have argued that European imports competed with and strangled African manufactures like cloth, while the import of luxury goods did nothing to spur African economies. But economic historians have shown that overseas trade comprised only a small part of most African economies before about 1870, and that on a *per capita* basis, the quantities of textiles, arms, alcohol, tobacco, and manufactures imported to Africa were far too small to have had a dramatic economic impact. Slaving was only one sector in economies that remained overwhelmingly agricultural. Still, conventional economic models posit that trade fuels economic growth because it promotes specialization, provides access to new inputs, and facilitates the transfer of technology. Putting aside the important qualifier that the trade goods coming from Africa were *human,* did the slave trade bring any significant economic *development* to Africa? The answer is largely "no." In contrast to Caribbean plantations, for instance, West Africa exported hardly any agricultural products, other than food for slave ships, often grown largely by slave villages. In 1726 King Agaja of Dahomey sent Bulfinch Lambe back to England in order to suggest to King George I that, instead of merely exporting Africans, Europeans should establish plantations in his kingdom for which he would supply slaves (see "Sources" at the end of this chapter). He never received a response. Similarly, the British Board of Trade in 1751 ordered the governor of Cape Coast Castle to stop cotton cultivation among local Africans, because "[t]he introduction of culture and industry among the Negroes is contrary to the known established policy of this country, there is no saying where this might stop, and . . . it might extend to tobacco, sugar and every other commodity which we now take from our colonies; and thereby the Africans, who now support themselves by wars, would become planters and their slaves be employed in the culture of these articles in Africa. . . ."

This reference to African planters' slaves is significant, for another major effect of the slave trade was to extend and transform slavery *in Africa.* Although a range of dependent relationships including slavery provided labor in pre-slave trade times (as mentioned in the Introduction), these systems of dependency were significantly altered by the growth of the Atlantic slave trade. External demand drew more people into the slave market, and slavery itself often became more rigid and onerous. At the height of the Atlantic slave trade, there were likely as many slaves held with Africa as there were in the Americas—some 3 to 5 million. Moreover, as the transatlantic slave trade gradually ended in the first half of the 19th century, the price of slaves on the African coast fell but the processes which supplied slaves remained in place. As slaves, especially men, came within the purchasing power of African buyers, the scope of African slavery expanded further, even though the total number of people captured may not have changed from before. Coastal plantations developed, producing food crops for palace populations and African markets, as well as cash crops like palm oil for export (as will be discussed further in Chapter 4). By 1850, nearly 10 million slaves toiled in Africa. Dependent relationships which had previously contained some flexibility now came to resemble forms of chattel slavery familiar to Europeans. By the end of the 19th century, this increasing similarity, coupled with violence which continued even after the Atlantic trade had been outlawed, ironically provided Europeans with an important rationalization for colonial conquest.

CONCLUSION

Although the overall effects of the Atlantic slave trade on Africa cannot be quantified precisely, they certainly were negative. A direct demographic drain of some 20 million people (including those captured or killed in Africa, those who died during the Middle Passage, and those who survived landing in the Americas) not only deprived other Africans of their economic productivity, political contributions, and social, kinship, and emotional ties; those captives' descendants were also lost. The old American slave spiritual lamenting the "many thousands gone" should really have mourned many *millions*. In exchange for those precious human lives, Africans received luxury goods that contributed little to their economies, and their involvement with the slave trade expanded slavery within Africa.

But African elites participated in the slave trade voluntarily, using it to increase their own power and wealth, as well as the strength of the groups they led. As long as their political communities and leaders stayed strong (through slave trading and other means), those who were considered "insiders" were generally protected, while societies and individuals outside the slaving frontiers faced terrible violence and insecurity. Africa's extreme political fragmentation, based on a high proportion of land to people, meant that relatively large numbers of "outsiders" lived within traveling distance of each other, vulnerable to enslavement particularly in times of war. Although some states stayed out of the trade and some individuals led resistance to it, slave trading was seductive. Kingdoms, chieftaincies, city-states, and the like could use the trade to protect or improve themselves while weakening their enemies, and at the same time benefiting kings and merchants personally as well. Like modern-day drug traffickers or environmental polluters, the elites who traded in human lives gained, even as society at large suffered.

SOURCES

■ Trade and Politics in the Kongo

Nzinga Mbemba, also known as Afonso I, became ruler of the Kongo kingdom in about 1506. Eager for foreign resources to help him maintain political power, Afonso welcomed Portuguese traders and missionaries. Kongo's relationship with the Portuguese included the sale of slaves, which increasingly destabilized the kingdom. The following excerpt is from a letter King Afonso wrote to King João III of Portugal about the slave trade in July 1526. It is part of a collection of 24 letters that Afonso and his Portuguese-educated, African secretaries sent to the kings of Portugal on a variety of issues.

Try to read through the complicated sentence structure of the letter and figure out what Afonso is saying. In his view, how have the availability of Portuguese goods and the presence of slave traders affected Kongo society? What seems to be the relationship between Portuguese goods and political power? Is Afonso criticizing the slave trade in general, or the particular way it was being conducted in Kongo?

Sir, Your Highness should know how our Kingdom is being lost in so many ways that it is convenient to provide for the necessary remedy, since this is caused by the excessive freedom given by your factors[3] and officials to the men and merchants who are allowed to come to this Kingdom to set up shops with goods and many things which have been prohibited by us, and which they spread throughout our Kingdoms and Domains in such an abundance that many of our vassals, whom we had in obedience, do not comply because they have the things in greater abundance than we ourselves; and it was with these things that we had them content and subjected under our vassalage and jurisdiction, so it is doing a great harm not only to the service of God, but the security and peace of our Kingdoms and State as well.

Source: Letter from Afonso I of Kongo to João III of Portugal, 1526. Translated and published in Basil Davidson, *The African Past: Chronicles from Antiquity to Modern Times* (Boston: Little Brown & Co., 1964), pp. 191–2.
[3]Agents.

And we cannot reckon how great the damage is, since the mentioned merchants are taking every day our natives, sons of the land and the sons of our noblemen and vassals and our relatives, because the thieves and men of bad conscience grab them wishing to have the things and wares of this Kingdom which they are ambitious of; they grab them and get them to be sold; and so great, Sir, is the corruption and licentiousness that our country is being completely depopulated. . . . That is why we beg of Your Highness to help and assist us in this matter, commanding your factors that they should not send here either merchants or wares, because it is *our will that in these Kingdoms there should not be any trade of slaves nor outlet for them.*[4]

■ Attempts to Raid for Slaves

Privateer John Hawkins was the first Englishman to seek slaves in West Africa, where he made three voyages in the mid-16th century. The small slave trade there was monopolized by the Portuguese, who had established peaceful commercial relations with African leaders. Hawkins, however, repeatedly attempted to seize captives by force.

As you read the following excerpts from Hawkins's account of his third voyage, consider these questions: What came of his attempt to raid for slaves at Cape Verde? How did he manage to secure more slaves after that? How effective were Hawkins's measures for capturing slaves? What was the goal of the African king with whom Hawkins allied?

. . . [We] arrived at Cape Verde the 18th of November, where we landed 150 men hoping to obtain some Negroes, where we got but few, and those with great hurt and damage to our men, which chiefly proceeded of their envenomed[5] arrows: and although in the beginning, [they] seemed to be but small hurts, yet there hardly escaped any that had blood drawn of them, and died in strange sort with their mouths shut,

---

[4]Emphasis in the original.
[5]Poisoned.
Source: John Hawkins on the Guinea coast, 1568. P. E. H. Hair (ed.), *Hawkins in Guinea, 1567–1568* (Leipzig: Institut für Afrikanistik, Universität Leipzig, 2000), pp. 25 and 64.

some ten days before he [*sic*] died, and after their wounds were whole, where I myself had one of the greatest wounds, yet thanks be to god escaped. . . .

From thence we passed the time upon the coast of Guinea searching with all diligence the rivers from Rio Grande unto the Sierra Leona until the 12th of January in which time we had not gotten together 150 Negroes. . . . But even in that present instant, there came to us a Negro sent from a King oppressed by other Kings his neighbors desiring our aid, with promise that as many negroes as by these wars might be obtained as well of his part as of ours should be at our pleasure whereupon we concluded to give aid, and sent 120 of our men which the 15th of January assaulted a town of the negroes of our Allies' adversaries . . . and put the inhabitants to flight where we took 250 persons men, women, and children and by our friend the king of our side there was taken 600 prisoners whereof we hoped to have had our choice: but the Negro (in which nation is seldom or never found truth) meant nothing less, for that night he removed his camp and prisoners, so that we were feign to content us with those few which we had gotten ourselves.

■ Dahomey and the Slave Trade

Bulfinch Lambe, an employee of the Royal African Company in its trading station at Jakin, the port of the kingdom of Allada, was seized and detained by the king of Allada in 1722. He was still held prisoner when Allada was conquered by the armies of Dahomey's King Agaja in 1724. Lambe was taken to the Dahomey capital of Abomey, where he remained captive until his release four years later. Then, perhaps at Lambe's opportunistic suggestion, Agaja sent Lambe to England to negotiate a commercial agreement with the Royal African Company—an agreement which was never made.

Source: Letter from King Agaja of Dahomey to King George I of England, 1726. Published in *The Parliamentary History of England, from the Earliest Period to the Year 1803*, Vol. XXVIII [1789–91] (London, 1816), 82–91 and republished in Robin Law, "Further Light on Bulfinch Lambe and the 'Emperor of Pawpaw:' King Agaja of Dahomey's Letter to King George I of England, 1726," *History in Africa* 17 (1990): 211–26. I have modernized and corrected spelling in a few cases.

The excerpt below is from a letter Lambe delivered in London in 1731. As you read it, consider the extent to which King Agaja's wealth and power were related to his participation in the slave trade. What foreign goods feature in this account? How important were they to the functioning of the kingdom, or to Agaja's personal position? What was the relationship between warfare, slavery, wealth, and power?

Great Prince; . . . .

. . . My grandfather was no warrior, and only enlarged his dominions by conquering one kingdom; my father nine; but my brother fought seventy-nine battles, in which he subdued several petty kingdoms; but myself have fought two hundred and nine battles, in which I have subdued many great kings and kingdoms, some of which are continually revolting and keeps me employed.

By computation I can send near 500,000 armed and well-skilled men to battle. . . . Both I and my predecessors were, and are, great admirers of fire arms, and have almost entirely left of the use of bows and arrows. . . .

We have a custom. . . . I am obliged to go out at different times in the year, and bestow great quantities of goods and money amongst the common people, and make sacrifices to our gods and forefathers, sometimes of slaves (which custom I have much broke) sometimes of horses, other times of oxen, and other creatures.

I very often besides love to go abroad about eight or ten miles an end. . . . When I am out I fix myself under some great shady tree; where I view what number of armed people I have ready in two or three hours; by this time up comes two or three hundred of my inferior wives, the chief favorites being about my person in sundry stations, some to fan and cool me, others to keep the flies away with whisks, others holding my arms, as guns, pistols, and saber, &c. others again holding parasols or umbrellas, which stand on the ground and make a canopy over my chair, and another to fill and light my pipe, which being done, I order the aforesaid bands of women to be unloaded, who have each a case of brandy, though clothed in crimson, green, blue, and black velvet and fine silks, and arrayed with great quantities of large coral (for my slaves buy me things of all nations.) . . . .

■ The Process of Enslavement in Angola

This description of the Portuguese Atlantic slave trade came from a Portuguese medical doctor with personal experience in Africa and Brazil. It was delivered as a lecture in Portugal in 1793.

In the following excerpt, Luiz Antonio de Oliveira Mendes describes the process of enslavement in Angola. What are the six ways Mendes delineates for becoming enslaved? What seem to be the most prevalent among them? To what extent is the process of enslavement governed by accepted rules of society? Who benefits, and who is vulnerable?

According to their laws there are six ways in which the black Africans can be enslaved. . . . [I]n each of their fortified places they choose judges from among themselves whom they call *sobas*, whose task it is to judge them. . . . The ultimate punishment on that continent is slavery, and in civil and criminal cases witnesses are questioned, and the debtor or adulterer condemned to slavery. He is at once put in irons, and awarded to the creditor or person who has been offended, who can sell him as his own, since as a result of the judgment and sentence, he will remain a slave as his form of punishment.

Among those people there is the custom that when someone is condemned to slavery, he can name others to suffer slavery in his place; however, this can only be done to persons over whom the condemned person has a claim. For example, he can name his children, his wives, or his nephews. . . .

When a black is seen stealing the harvest or fruits of another, and taking what is not his, the crime having been proved in the *soba's* presence, he is condemned to slavery. . . .

When a kingdom makes war against another kingdom and is victorious, possessing the right to kill their conquered enemies, this right is transformed into that of slavery, and thus the captives can be

---

Source: Luiz Antonio de Oliveira Mendes, 1793. Luiz Antonio de Oliveira Mendes, *Discurso academico ao programa: determiner com todos os seus symptomas as doenças agudas, e chronicas, que mais frequentemente accometem os pretos recem tirados da Africa* (Lisbon: Real Academia, 1812), in Robert Edgar Conrad, *Children of God's Fire: A Documentary History of Black Slavery in Brazil* (Princeton: Princeton University Press, 1983), pp. 16–17.

bartered. This is how in this center of heathenism the rights of war are interpreted.

The fifth way in which the free man is innocently brought into slavery is by force and treachery. Certain pirates among them deceptively persuade others to go with them to certain places, and there rushing upon those they wish to enslave, they seize them and then sell them to backlanders[6] when these are in certain places to barter for slaves, their trade fairs, for example. . . .

Sometimes it happens that needy family fathers, who have not themselves been sentenced, willfully desiring to punish their children and concubines, sell their own concubines and children to the backlanders, thus delivering them into slavery. . . .

Having been reduced to slavery in Africa, either because he was so condemned, or as a result of piracy and treachery, this once free black human being is the most unhappy person imaginable. . . .

---

[6]Portuguese or Afro-Portuguese traders based in the interior.

CHAPTER

3

How Did Enslaved People Cope?

THE *HENRIETTA MARIE*

In 1972, a team of treasure-hunters discovered a shipwreck near Key West, Florida. Instead of coins and jewels, however, these and subsequent divers found material remains of intense human suffering. On the ocean floor lay over 80 pairs of iron shackles, some large enough to embrace a grown man's ankle, some so small that they only could have held the narrow wrist of a child. The undersea explorers also found a massive cauldron, in which stew or gruel evidently was cooked for hundreds of people, along with iron bars used as currency and weights, stamped in London, designed to measure trading goods. Although most shipwrecks are nearly impossible to identify specifically, this one yielded a cracked bronze bell bearing the ship's name, the *Henrietta Marie*. Shipping records confirmed what the divers had already surmised: that the *Henrietta Marie* carried slaves from Africa to the Caribbean. The ship's second and last slaving voyage began in

London in 1699 and continued with trading at New Calabar, in the Bight of Biafra. After crossing the Atlantic, the vessel landed at Jamaica, where 190 African captives—out of just over 200 originally purchased—were sold. The *Henrietta Marie* sank in 1700, loaded with sugar and other colonial products on the third leg of its triangular journey, en route back to England.

Unique as an archaeological find, since few identifiable slave shipwrecks have been explored, the *Henrietta Marie* is also in some ways emblematic of the more than 30,000 transatlantic slaving voyages that took place between 1518 and the 1860s. The relics found on board attest to the ship's dual functions, as both a trading vessel and a floating prison. They make evident the double status of the enslaved Africans held below decks: they were captives and commodities. But the materials contained on a slave ship primarily reflect the worldview of those who outfitted it—the financial backers and the captain—and offer only limited insights into the experiences of the captive Africans.

The prisoners who crossed the Atlantic on the *Henrietta Marie*, and the thousands of other slave ships, most often began their miserable journeys far from coastal ports. The trauma of capture and initial enslavement was followed by separation from loved ones, long inland marches, and vulnerability to injury, illness, and malnutrition. At the ports, prisoners were stuffed into dungeons, warehouses, or pens to await further horrors upon meeting European traders: degrading examinations, excruciating branding, and tortuous rides through the surf toward the ships waiting at anchor. Relics from slave ships suggest the captives' determination to resist: shackles, weapons, and the ship's architecture itself were part of a struggle to control prisoners who attempted to flee or fight back. But they only hint at the slaves' suffering in the cramped, stifling holds, with inadequate provisions, ravaged by illness and terrorized by torture. And the remains from slave ships offer no information about the fate and struggles of the ships' prisoners after their maritime passages were over.

Although traded as chattel, the Africans who disembarked from slave ships entered the societies of the Americas as people bearing distinct cultures. They spoke a variety of African languages, practiced specific African forms of worship (including Islam and Christianity), and were used to particularly African styles of social organization and artistic production. The process by which newly arrived Africans and their descendants became African American, Afro-Brazilian, Afro-Cuban, and so forth is still inadequately understood by historians and other researchers. Yet it is clear that as they struggled for survival, enslaved Africans built communities and reshaped their worldviews in the Americas, combining the cultures they brought with them with the new circumstances they endured.

PASSAGES ON LAND

In addition to violence and alienation from their loved ones, enslaved Africans shared the experience of mobility. Generally their forced migrations began in the interior, where they were captured in warfare, kidnapped, handed over for payment on a debt, or arrested by local authorities. The traumatic conditions of enslavement often injured or weakened new captives, in spite of the fact that buyers preferred fit, healthy slaves. Even if enslaved people avoided physical harm in their initial capture, their long, hard marches, followed by confinement in coastal forts or barracoons (crude wooden pens), weakened their bodies and battered their spirits.

We can only imagine the anguish experienced by those who were seized, enslaved, and headed for the coast. As the English explorer Mungo Park, who traveled to Africa in the late 18th century, remarked about a young girl who was sold, "Never was a face of serenity more suddenly changed into one of the deepest distress. . . . The terror she manifested in having the load put upon her head and the rope fastened around her neck, and the sorrow with which she bade adieu to her companions were truly affecting." Venture Smith was captured when an enemy army overran his homeland in the 1730s (see the first source at the end of this chapter). After his father was killed by the raiders, he, his mother, and other members of his community were forcibly herded 400 miles toward the coast. "All the march I had very hard tasks imposed on me," he later recounted, "which I must perform on pain of punishment. I was obliged to carry on my head a large flat stone used for grinding our corn, weighing, as I should suppose, as much as twenty-five pounds; besides victuals, mat and cooking utensils. Though I was pretty large and stout of my age, yet these burdens were very grievous to me, being only six years and a half old."

Unknown numbers of captives died of their injuries, illnesses, deprivation, and heartbreak during the weeks and months in which they trudged toward coastal ports. Joseph Miller's study of the slave trade between West Central Africa and Brazil suggests that as many as one-third of the captives died between enslavement in the interior and their arrival at the shore roughly six months later. An additional 10 percent, this historian concluded, perished in the filthy, disease-ridden, open-air barracoons of Luanda and Benguela, where large numbers of slaves squatted naked in the dirt for days or weeks before being forced onto transatlantic ships. Such calculations suggest that overall, something like 20 million Africans were captured as slaves and channeled toward the coast. Of those, some 12 million survived to be loaded onto ships bound for the Americas.

The newly captured did not leave their homes and communities willingly. Although people who fled the slave processions (called *coffles*, from the Arabic word for "caravan") did not leave written records, the measures used by African and European slave dealers to prevent escape suggest that it was often attempted (see Figure 3.1). On the long trek to the coastal ports, captives were frequently manacled and harnessed to one another by neck irons, heavy ropes, or wooden yokes. Similar precautions were taken with prisoners at the coastal forts and pens. Visitors to the West African castles and trade forts today are struck not merely by the menacing gloom of the dungeons, which let out on to the sea, but also by the proliferation of ring-bolts in their walls—part of the hardware of prison security.

FIGURE 3.1 A *coffle* en route to the coast

African families who could do so looked for their relatives, pooled resources, walked to the slave ships, and sometimes offered human ransoms in order to free their loved ones. Samuel Ajayi Crowther, who was enslaved as a child in the 19th-century Yoruba wars (and whose account is one of the sources for Chapter 4), noticed people "in search of their relations, to set at liberty as many as they had the means of redeeming." Individual captives were difficult to find, however, as Ayuba Suleyman Diallo (later Job ben Solomon) of Senegambia found out. In 1731, the young husband and father, son of an Islamic cleric, traveled to the Gambia to sell slaves and buy paper. On his way home, he was captured and sold to the same ship captain he had dealt with earlier. Through acquaintances he sent word to his father and, as a result, a caravan was sent with several slaves to take his place. The men arrived too late, though, and Diallo was shipped to Maryland.

Nearly all captives who survived the passage to the coast waited there in forts, warehouses, and barracoons for European purchasers to arrive. Crowded into dank, rancid enclosures, they were guarded aggressively and provisioned only minimally. In the late 18th-century Gambia, Mungo Park observed, captives could be "distributed among the neighbouring villages until a slave ship arrives." There, "the poor wretches are kept constantly fettered, two and two of them being chained together, and employed in the labours of the field; and I am sorry to add, are very scantily fed, as well as harshly treated." After several weeks or even months, strange-looking Europeans appeared, and a new phase of the captives' horrors began. Individually or in small groups, they were subjected to humiliating and invasive physical inspections before their purchasers began the process of haggling over prices. Once the deal was finalized, a captive would be seized and held tightly while his purchaser's mark was seared into his flesh with a red-hot branding iron. Some prisoners endured such tortures multiple times: in Angola, at least three separate brands indicated that a given captive had been purchased, counted by a tax collector, and hastily baptized in accordance with Portuguese regulations.

Boarding the ships was chaotic and terrifying, particularly for prisoners who had never seen the sea before. The Dutch slave trader Willem Bosman recorded that those captives whose clothing had survived their ordeals so far were stripped, and "came aboard stark naked as well women as men; in which condition they are obliged to continue, if the master of the Ship is not so charitable (which he commonly is) as to bestow something on them to cover their nakedness." In this degrading and uncomfortable condition, slaves made jarring, soggy passages on canoes or small boats through the surf to the large ships waiting at anchor. Ottobah Cugoano, taken from the Gold Coast at the age of 13, recalled, "when a vessel arrived to conduct us away to the ship, it was a most horrible scene; there was nothing to be heard but rattling of chains, smacking of whips, and the groans and cries of our fellow men." His contemporary Olaudah Equiano, whose account of fainting on boarding a slave ship began Chapter 1, shared a fear common to enslaved Africans, that the European traders were cannibals: "When I looked round the ship too and saw a large furnace of copper boiling, and a multitude of black people of every description chained together, every one of their countenances expressing dejection and sorrow, I no longer doubted of my fate. . . . I asked if we were not to be eaten by those white men with horrible looks, red faces and long hair?" In every part of Africa, Europeans were regarded as cannibals, an impression seemingly confirmed when captives saw the huge cauldrons kept on deck. Some Africans believed Europeans would make gunpowder out of their bones. In the Bight of Benin, rumors spread that the cowry shells Europeans paid for slaves grew on the carcasses of captives thrown overboard. In Angola, slaves believed that the Portuguese distilled red wine from the blood of Africans, boiled their brains to make the soft, white cheese imported from Brazil, and burned their bodies to make gunpowder from the ashes. All of these ideas were ways of understanding that Europeans did not abide by the normal rules of civilized societies.

PASSAGES AT SEA

The term "Middle Passage" refers to the second leg of a three-part circuit of exchange between Europe, Africa, the Americas, and back to Europe. It is the most notorious aspect of the Atlantic slave trade, because the double identity of captives as both trade goods and people emerged horrifically in the teeming holds of slave ships. As the British abolitionist and parliamentarian William Wilberforce put it, "Never can so much misery be found condensed in so small a place as in a slave ship during the Middle Passage." Yet the miserable conditions for slaves reflected rational, economic calculations on the part of ship captains and their European employers. Though it might seem that the arrangements on a slave ship were chaotic, with the slavers cramming Africans into the hold and quickly sailing off, the slave trade was in fact a highly organized business driven by a specific goal: to get the costly cargo of slaves across the ocean with as few losses as possible. Otherwise, profit was impossible. Such economic calculations rested on a vision of slaves as commodities whose humanity was irrelevant, particularly given the racist justifications for African slavery. But the humanity of enslaved people was always evident, in their vulnerability to injury, sickness, and death; in their ability to cope and survive; and, as slavers were well aware, in their determination to resist.

During the peak decades of the trade, ships were specially built or adapted for slave cargoes. The maximum capacity was calculated carefully and sometimes diagramed on charts, with slaving ships generally measuring between 50 and 125 feet long and 8 to 15 feet wide, averaging 100–300 tons. Although they carried merchandise from Europe to Africa, they were each also capable of holding slaves in numbers ranging from fewer than 100 to more than 500. While the trading took place on African shores, carpenters refitted the vessels lying at anchor, transforming them from merchant ships to floating prisons. They installed platforms between decks to hold slaves, typically building two levels, one above the other, on either side of the ship, separated by a central passageway. Partitions were erected to separate the sexes and age groups and, Europeans hoped, retard the spread of slave insurrections. Drawings for slave ships show that each captive was allocated 5–7 square feet below decks, with less than two feet of headroom. The only position possible for prisoners in the holds was to lie on their sides, fit against each other like spoons in a drawer, unable to sit up or move much at all. As Mahommad Baquaqua, a West African Muslim taken to Brazil in the 1840s, recalled,

> We were thrust into the hold of the vessel in a state of nudity, the males being crammed on one side, and the females on the other; the hold was so low that we could not stand up, but were obliged to crouch upon the floor or sit down; day and night were the same to us, sleep being denied us from the confined position of our bodies, and we became desperate through suffering and fatigue.

Men were chained together in pairs, right hands and feet to left hands and feet, so that in order to walk or lay down it was necessary to coordinate movements. When the weather was rough they were kept below for long periods, tossing and sliding as the wood of the platforms rubbed their skin raw. Some mornings, after nights of bad weather, crew members entering the holds would find two slaves manacled together, one dead and one living.

Between the large numbers of people crammed into unventilated spaces and the intestinal diseases that ravaged them, the holds of slave vessels became filthy cesspools. "The closeness of the place, and the heat of the climate," Equiano wrote, "added to the number in the ship, which was so crowded that each had scarcely room to turn himself, almost suffocated us. This produced copious perspirations, so that the air soon became unfit for respiration, from a variety of loathsome smells, and brought on a sickness among the slaves, of which many died." The French slave trader Jean Barbot noted that sometimes the heat and lack of oxygen on the lower decks of slave ships were so intense that "the surgeons would faint away and the candles would not burn." Although buckets for human excrement might be set up at the end of platforms, it was nearly impossible for chained slaves to get to them. Below decks, the muck and stench from blood, sweat, urine, feces, and vomit overwhelmed any attempts at cleanliness. Crews were ordered to mop up the mess, scrub down the ship, and clear the air below decks with vinegar, whitewash, or tar. They made some efforts to bathe slaves by tossing seawater on them, in spite of the pain salt water inflicted on open wounds. Ships downwind of slaving vessels could identify them by their odor even when they were far out of sight.

Ship captains had to calculate how much food and water were necessary for captives and crew, based on estimates of the voyage's length. At African ports they purchased most of their provisions: local starches, beans, and casks of fresh water, but few fruits or vegetables. On board, crews fed their prisoners once or twice a day, typically in communal bowls which the strong could dominate at the expense of the weak. Fresh water rations were tightly controlled, as on Mahommad Baquaqua's ship, where "we suffered very much for want of water, but were denied all we needed. A pint a day was allowed, and no more . . ." Under the best of circumstances, slaves faced chronic undernutrition and thirst; but when voyages ran longer than expected or captains had planned poorly, hunger and dehydration became acute, endangering the slaves' lives and the slavers' profits. On the notorious English ship *Zong*, shortages of supplies even led to murder.

The *Zong* left West Africa for Jamaica in March 1783, carrying 440 slaves and 14 crew members. As the Atlantic crossing dragged on much longer than expected, the ship ran short of water and people began to die. By November, 60 slaves and 7 members of the crew had perished, while many others were ill and not likely to live. Each slave death reduced the profits of the voyage, but the captain knew that at least the *Zong*'s human cargo was partially insured: if captives died by natural causes there would be no insurance payments, but if they were lost in suppression of a revolt, the voyage's financial backers (and ultimately the captain himself) would receive compensation. On the captain's orders, 54 Africans were chained together and then thrown overboard. Another 78 were drowned over the next two days. The incident came to light only because insurance adjusters disputed the claim and brought the case to court. Though no murder charges were filed, 18th-century British justice prevailed, and the insurance company was not obligated to pay.

In addition to food and water, captives needed some form of exercise if they were to remain healthy at sea. Women and children frequently were allowed to move freely on deck, but slave traders brought out adult men only at specific times, including for exercise. With the prodding of a whip and occasionally a drum, accordion, or fiddle for accompaniment, they forced slaves to "dance" on deck. The slaves' shackles, kept on as a security measure, made their macabre "dance" limited and painful. Sometimes ships' crews took sadistic delight in such spectacles. In 1792, for instance, Captain John Kimber was tried in the British Court of Admiralty over the death of a 15-year-old female slave taken on his ship from New Calabar to the West Indies. According to the prosecution, Kimber tortured the young woman to death because she had refused to dance naked on the deck of his ship. He was ultimately acquitted, the jury having concluded that the girl died of disease, not maltreatment (see Figure 3.2).

Women experienced the Middle Passage, like slavery itself, differently than men. On average, almost twice as many men as women filled slave ships, and children made up a significant minority of the prisoners. Babies, conceived in freedom or in any of the many passages of slavery, were born on slave ships; others were carried by

The ABOLITION of the SLAVE TRADE.
Or the Inhumanity of Dealers in human flesh exemplified in Capt.ⁿ Kimber's treatment of a young Negro Girl of 15 for her Virgin Modesty.

FIGURE 3.2 Engraved colored print by George Cruikshank, published in London in 1792 and captioned, "The Abolition of the Slave Trade, Or the inhumanity of dealers in human flesh exemplified in Captn. Kimber's treatment of a young Negro girl of 15 for her virjen [*sic*] modesty."

Source: Library of Congress, Prints and Photographs Division, British Cartoon Collection, LC-USZ62-6204.

valiant mothers who tried to protect them. Although women and children occupied quarters separate from enslaved men and spent extra time on deck, their special treatment offered little comfort. Nearly all firsthand accounts of the Middle Passage concur with Cugoano that "... it was common for the dirty filthy sailors to take the African women and lie upon their bodies...." Such incidents came to light only occasionally, as when Second Captain Philippe Liot committed multiple rapes on a French ship in the 1770s. The physical and emotional damage he inflicted on two slaves, a woman who broke two teeth attempting to resist and a ten-year-old girl who was assaulted three nights in a row, reduced their sale prices in St. Domingue. This economic loss, compounded when the adult victim died two weeks later, explains why the rapist was reported by his captain. Generally, sailors considered the rape of captive women to be an unremarkable fringe benefit.

Some slaves attempted suicide in their depression, fear, and anger, and perhaps in hopes that death would return them to their homes. Ships' crews erected netting around the upper deck to prevent slaves from jumping into the ocean. Equiano said he would have taken the opportunity himself if not prevented, and told of two Igbo men on his ship who, despite being chained together, managed to get through the netting into the water. Slaves were beaten severely for attempting suicide, as well as for disobeying (often incomprehensible) orders or taking any action construed as resistance. Even when it did not lead to suicide, depression was so common that contemporary Europeans called it "fixed melancholy" and took special steps to deal with it. Equiano reported being severely flogged for not eating, despite his young age. Others had food jammed down their throats, sometimes enduring broken teeth in the process. Slaves who tried to starve themselves were tortured, or force-fed with the help of a contraption called a *speculum orum*, which pried the mouth open. (See the second source at the end of this chapter.)

Unrelenting physical force governed the operation of slave ships. Crews, comprised of poor people who sometimes had been "impressed" (kidnapped) into service, were themselves vulnerable to violence from the captain, although their relative powerlessness did not temper their own abuse of the slaves. Slaves no doubt hated their captors, and they had few personal ties to inhibit their attempts to escape. Although gaps remain in the historical record, historian David Richardson estimates that perhaps as many as 10 percent of slave ships experienced an insurrection. Another historian, Eric Robert Taylor, has uncovered evidence of 493 shipboard revolts. Stunningly, some 25 percent of them brought freedom for at least some of the insurrectionists involved; and in the 18th century alone, revolts in which at least some of the slaves freed themselves occurred at a rate of more than one per year. In spite of these heroic successes, however, slave ships' crews managed to put down most rebellions, often at the cost of many slaves' lives. Captured ringleaders were executed with extreme cruelty to intimidate the others. As Cugoano recalled, ". . . when we found ourselves at last taken away, death was more preferable than life, and a plan was concerted amongst us that we might burn and blow up the ship, and to perish all together in the flames. But we were betrayed . . . the discovery was likewise a cruel and bloody scene."

Perhaps captives' attempted revolts, unsuccessful as they usually were, were not completely futile, however. The possibility of revolts caused owners of slave ships to invest in additional crew—about twice as many as on similar merchant marine vessels—and hardware like firearms, swivel guns, and cannons. Richardson argues that these expenses increased the costs of slaving voyages, which in turn affected the overall magnitude of the slave trade by raising prices for American purchasers. Between 1680 and 1800, according to this historian, without shipboard resistance by Africans the number of slaves shipped across the Atlantic could have been 9 percent greater than it actually was. Thus, Africans who died fighting slave traders, as well as those who resisted unsuccessfully and survived to work on plantations, saved perhaps another 600,000 Africans from being shipped to America during the peak years of the trade and 1 million during its whole history.

The final experience of many of the Africans chained below decks was death, in numbers so large that the Portuguese knew slave ships as "floating tombs" (*tumbeiros*) and sharks followed them to get at the bodies thrown overboard. Suicide and tortures destroyed captives, but the most common killer was disease. There were no cures during the slave trade era for the bacterial infections that caused diarrhea, dysentery, and ultimately dehydration. Gastrointestinal disorders, yellow fever, and malaria accounted for the vast majority of Middle Passage deaths, while smallpox and other epidemic diseases could break out especially on long voyages with inadequate provisions. In the 16th and early 17th centuries, as many as 20 percent of the captives sailing from Africa to the Americas perished.

Traders were less concerned about African lives than about how such high death rates affected their profits. In the 18th century, for instance, the French Company of the Indies gave its captains a bonus of six *livres* per slave if mortality during the crossing was less than 5 percent, three *livres* for less than 10 percent, two *livres* for less than 15 percent, and one *livre* for less than 20 percent, which was still considered an acceptable mortality rate. During the peak years of the slave trade, economic calculations motivated merchants of all nationalities to improve slave survival rates during the Middle Passage. Ship sizes were standardized, with the typical vessel larger than in previous eras, because about 300 slaves were deemed to be an optimal cargo. Faster ships reduced the length of time at sea, from an average Atlantic crossing of two to three months in the early 16th century to roughly one month by the time the trade ended in the mid-19th century. Captains followed general guidelines for providing adequate food and water and keeping ships cleaner and better ventilated than before. Such efforts reduced average mortality from 20 percent to less than 10 percent by the late 1700s. Because so much of the trade was conducted during the period with the lowest death rates, the average rate of loss per voyage during the entire period of the slave trade was 12 percent. Still, mortality for transatlantic ships carrying convicts, contract laborers, military troops, and fresh immigrants dropped far faster and to lower levels than slave ships. The desire for profit, combined with European traders' racist notions that African slaves did not qualify for humanitarian concerns, made the Middle Passage an intense combination of market rationality and human suffering.

AFRICAN CULTURES IN THE NEW WORLD

For the 10.8 million heroic Africans who survived the Middle Passage, reaching land must have brought some relief: fresh food and water were now available, and finally it was possible to move around. But arrival in the Americas meant new hardships. Ships and their cargoes were inspected for evidence of disease by coastal authorities, who could impose quarantine and delay disembarkation for several weeks. Once ashore, slaves were put on auction, where they faced new physical examinations and one or more additional brandings. Many were separated from relatives and new friends. After their sale, some had to endure another voyage or a long over-land journey to their final destinations. In most cases, the weakened, exhausted new arrivals ended up on plantations, where they faced an unfamiliar disease environment and new work regimes. They had new masters whose language likely was foreign to them, new companions, and new challenges to their survival.

West Indian planters referred to slaves' initial adjustment to the New World as "seasoning." In the Brazilian trade, according to Joseph Miller's figures, some 5 percent of captives died during the process of sale in Brazil, with another 15 percent of the remainder perishing during the first year of "seasoning." In the Caribbean sugar colonies, as many as half of the newly arrived slaves died within three years of their arrival. Perhaps a quarter of the slaves who came to 18th-century Virginia died within their first year, as did roughly a third in the Carolina low country.

Miserable as the process of adjustment surely was, some newly arrived slaves at least endured it with companions from their home areas, larger ethno-linguistic groups, or even slave ships. Through their shared experiences of intense suffering, shipmates formed bonds of friendship, sometimes even in spite of their origins in different, potentially antagonistic, ethnic groups. In Brazil, Central Africans recognized such connections, using the Kimbundu/Kikongo word *malungu* (sometimes rendered as *melungo*) to describe people who were considered as close as kin because they had made the journey from Africa together. Captives in the English-speaking Americas retained such bonds as well, and "shipmates" designated people who had near-kinship ties which endured for generations. Because many slaves, particularly those destined for large plantations, were purchased in lots, they were likely to have at least some companionship in their misery. And because most ships collected their slaves from a particular African region, rather than "coasting" from place to place, new arrivals in the Americas could often engage in at least some communication with each other.

If captives disembarked from slave ships as Africans—speaking distinct African languages, practicing African religions, accustomed to political and social structures they had lived with in Africa—over time they and their descendants became *Creoles*, a term that sometimes refers to the American-born and more generally implies cultural mixing. Africans in the Americas had two cultural adjustments to make: to the other Africans, of diverse origins, enduring slavery with them, and to the Euro-Americans who made up the ruling class. For decades, historians were convinced that slave life was so harsh, and the enslaved population so ethnically diverse, that "creolization" (i.e., the process of acculturation) took place rapidly. Specific African languages, religions, and folkways were quickly lost, replaced either by elements of European culture or by new ways of doing things that combined features from various African and non-African origins. More recently, other scholars have argued that African individuals and groups maintained specific aspects of their home cultures in American slavery. These historians acknowledge the inevitable cultural mixing that took place between slaves with different African homelands as well as between black and white, but they suggest that this process occurred more slowly and later than was previously assumed. In the short term, recognizable cultural forms from particular African locations persisted throughout the Americas. And over the long term, as Africans did engage in cultural transformation, they still kept traces of their origins with them. When Africans spoke European languages, they maintained some African inflections; when they became familiar with Euro-American Christianity, they transformed it; and when they confronted white supremacy through an evolving shared identity as "black," they sometimes belonged to more "ethnic" or "national" associations as well.

Although some scholars have argued that African slave populations in the Americas were extremely ethnically and linguistically diverse, new research based on the slave trade database indicates that, like European migrants, Africans in the New World formed distinct ethnic blocs. Four-fifths of the slaves who arrived in southeastern Brazil, for instance, came from West Central Africa, while a similar proportion of captives brought to Bahia (northeastern Brazil) after 1680 were from the Bight of Benin. Nearly two-thirds of the Africans brought to Louisiana in the French slave trade came from Senegambia. The ethnic composition of particular slave populations could also change over time, as suppliers shifted their areas of concentration within Africa. For example, for the first 150 years of the slave trade, more than seven out of ten slaves coming to the Americas were from West Central Africa, largely from Kongo, Angola, and Ndongo. That means that from the 16th through the 17th centuries there was likely to have been significant cultural continuity among the enslaved populations of Mexico, Peru, and northeastern Brazil, the major destinations of these slaves. Three-quarters of all slaves in Jamaica before 1725 probably came from the Gold Coast and the culturally similar Bight of Benin. Then over the next 80 years, the proportion from the Bight of Benin fell significantly and that from the Gold Coast fell gradually, replaced by imports from the Bight of Biafra and, less significantly, the northern network of West Central Africa. In a pattern similar to those of European colonial settlements, most African slave populations in the Americas began with migrants from a single area and later drew a greater ethno-linguistic range of occupants. In most regions, African ethnic diversity developed over time.

When new Africans arrived in the Americas, European owners, already enslaved Africans, and their American-born descendants identified them according to their "nation"—a designation based roughly on geographic origin and linguistic group (see Figure 3.3). But such "nations" were New World inventions, varying in their names and specific connotations from place to place. Throughout the Americas, captives from Central Africa were identified as Angolas and Kongos, although in Brazil these categories were subdivided further. Slaves

FIGURE 3.3 "Black slaves, from different nations." These engravings, showing the hairstyles, facial markings, and jewelry of different African ethnic groups, were taken from drawings made by a French traveler during his residence in Brazil from 1816 to 1831.

Source: Jean Baptiste Debret, *Voyage Pittorsque et Historique au Bresil* (Paris, 1834–39), vol. 2, plate 22, p. 75 and vol. 2, plat 56, p. 113. (Copy in the John Carter Brown Library at Brown University.)

exported from Bight of Benin ports were designated as, among others, Yarriba, Foulah, and Hausa in English-speaking areas, Lucumí in Cuba, and Nagô, Guiné, Mâle, Jeje, and Whydah in Brazil. "Nations" corresponded only roughly to existing states in Africa, which were undergoing change themselves during the period of the slave trade. In Brazil, for instance, the term *Nagô* identified a group of Africans even before the word *Yoruba* came to identify their countrymen in Africa. Europeans believed that Africans from given geographically and linguistically based "nations" shared certain attributes, and based decisions about slave purchase and employment on such stereotypes. English planters favored "Coromantees" (people from the Gold Coast) for their reputed initiative, hardiness, and bravery, for instance, but also feared their tendency to revolt. French planters in St. Domingue distinguished at least 20 different African peoples, assigning different types of work to members of different nations. At the same time, and perhaps more importantly, "nation" was a salient marker of identity for slaves themselves, and among other slaves. By identifying with particular nations, or ethnicities, Africans formed bonds within and across plantations and individual work sites, organizing for mutual aid, emotional support, and social release. Although enslaved people interacted with others outside of their "nation," shared membership in "national" groups provided a major basis for social networks and allowed Africans to maintain languages, beliefs, songs, music, and rituals from their homelands.

One of the strongest signs of ethnic identity was the African name preserved along with the one the master imposed. For Africans a personal name had special symbolic power, connoting the circumstances of birth, the individual's position in the family lineage, the family's prosperity, and other traits. Although Africans in the Americas were given European names, they often identified themselves to friends and relatives by their original names from their homelands. Gwendolyn Midlo Hall's database of Louisiana slaves contains over 10,000 individuals (out of nearly 92,000) with African names, not including the large numbers with names designating ethnicity, like Louis Congo or Samba Bambara. African-born slaves not only retained their own names, at least privately, they also passed them on to their children born in the Americas.

While members of African "nations" came together in various ways throughout the Americas, in Brazil and Cuba they also formed officially recognized Catholic lay brotherhoods. Brotherhoods were ethnic mutual-aid societies: they offered loans and donations; they bought members' freedom; and they organized and financed burials and masses for the dead. Brotherhoods were also centers for culture and leisure. On Christian holidays, especially the brotherhood's patron saint's day, the members gave parties and costume balls that included coronations of African kings and queens. Cuba, similarly, had *cabildos de Naciones*, which elected officials, made loans, and even acquired property. The Mina, Mandingo, Lucumí, Ashanti, and Carabalí each had their own *cabildo*. Less publicly, Africans in various ethnic groupings maintained and re-created burial practices, coming-of-age rituals, secret oaths, weddings, naming ceremonies, and divination practices from their homelands. Senegambians and others who were Muslims endeavored to maintain dietary restrictions and their daily regimens of prayers in non-Muslim environments. Some slaves in Brazil utilized specific Central African, especially Mbundu, ritual practices and beliefs, including divination, ordeals, ritual burials, dietary restrictions, and cures, as a way of addressing their condition. Throughout the Americas, enslaved Africans also sang songs from their homelands and made African-inspired musical instruments resembling lutes, harps, and guitars, as well as various kinds of drums.

"National" connections helped to organize resistance, particularly in the maroon communities formed by escaped slaves in the first two centuries of slavery in the Americas. By the mid-1600s, runaways had formed hundreds of autonomous societies in the Americas, called *kilombos* in Brazil (the same term applied to Imbangala camps in Central Africa, as described in Chapter 2) and *palenques* in Spanish America. Located in otherwise uninhabited areas, as in the "Dismal Swamp" of North Carolina and Virginia, or close to Native American populations, as in Florida and Honduras, maroon communities held between a few dozen and several thousand people. In the hills and forests of Jamaica, mainly Coromantee slaves (from the Gold Coast) founded maroon settlements during and after the English seizure of the island from the Spaniards in the 17th century. After protracted fighting, maroons under the leadership of a general named Cudjoe made a formal agreement with the British that granted them a section of the island as their own in exchange for peace, military aid against invaders, and help suppressing slave rebellions. Similar treaties with the large maroon population in Surinam (Dutch Guiana) recognized their possession of large inland regions.

In northeastern Brazil, the largest and longest-lasting maroon settlement, Palmares, was formed and led by slaves from Angola (see the third source at the end of this chapter). Lasting from around 1605 to 1695, Palmares ("palm forests") was more an independent state than a community of runaways, with a peak population of perhaps as many as 30,000 individuals. It was one of at least ten major maroon communities in colonial Brazil, some of which were combined settlements of Africans and the indigenous population. Although initially founded by African-born runaways, over time Palmares was inhabited by many who were born in Brazil (and even born in Palmares). The *kilombo* was composed of ten federated political units, each of which owed allegiance to the *Ganga-Zumba*, or "great lord." As a haven for runaways, Palmares was such a threat to Portuguese interests that it endured approximately one military attack every 15 months between 1672 and 1694. It was finally destroyed when 6,000 troops laid siege to the settlement for six weeks, after which the Palmares ruler Zumbi was captured and decapitated, his head publicly displayed as proof of his human vulnerability.

During the 18th and 19th centuries, slaves still tended to organize resistance struggles with members of their own nations. Coromantees were identified as leaders in several Caribbean slave revolts, as well as in conspiracies in 1712 and 1741 in New York. Kongo slaves formed a core group of those who revolted at Stono, South Carolina, in 1739 and in St. Domingue as part of the more widespread Haitian Revolution. "Mina" slaves (from the western Bight of Benin, in and around Whydah) at Pointe Coupée, Louisiana were accused of conspiring to revolt in 1791. The 1835 Mâle Revolt in Bahia was spearheaded by Muslim slaves from the Yoruba and Hausa ethnic groups of modern Nigeria. But although conspiracies were led by members of particular "nations," they often appealed to broader segments of enslaved populations. An antislavery plot in Cuba in 1811 was led by the leader of the Cabildo Shangó Tedum (Yoruba), with support of the Cabildo de Mandingo, the Cabildo de Ashanti, and the Cabildo de Mina Guagui. And maroon communities generally did not bar potential members on the basis of their ethnicity, even when they were organized around concepts of African nationhood. Their common condition brought the African-descended of many origins to an increasingly shared identity.

Creolization in the Americas varied over time and place. It was probably fastest and most significant in English-speaking North America, where the slave population was the first to reproduce itself naturally and the overall numbers of African imports were small compared to the ultimate size of the slave labor force. In Brazil, by contrast, the Atlantic slave trade ended late (not until 1850), and ethno-linguistically distinct blocs persisted in the African-descended population into the 20th century. In all the slave societies of the Western Hemisphere, however, American-born slaves came to outnumber those with memories of Africa, and African cultural elements merged with each other and with those from Europe. Increasingly over time, members of African nations lived, worked, and interacted with creole slaves and European owners and overseers. For example, the Catholic lay brotherhood in Salvador, Bahia (northeastern Brazil), called Our Lady of the Rosary, was exclusively Angolan in its 17th-century origins. Beginning in the second half of the 18th century, the organization started admitting non-Angolans, especially Jejes (from around Whydah) and Creoles. By the first decade of the 19th century, Jejes had become numerically dominant in the brotherhood, but the organization's bylaws prohibited them from serving on the board of directors, which remained restricted to Angolans and Creoles. Jejes also had their own brotherhood in Salvador, called Lord Sweet Jesus of the Needy, Redeemer of the Black Man, while Our Lady of Good Death was the brotherhood organized by Nagôs. At the same time, though, Jejes and Nagôs belonged to brotherhoods originally established by other Africans. Similarly, slave rebellions in the late 18th and early 19th centuries included members of particular nations in collaboration with American-born slaves. The Haitian Revolution, for example, was led by Toussaint L'Ouverture and other Creoles but also included semi-autonomous bands of West Central Africans and others, who did not speak French and communicated in their own languages.

Ultimately, African languages in the Americas were all replaced by European or creole tongues. Although Africans could use their own languages with others who spoke them, they also had to find ways of communicating with slaves of different origins and with Europeans. For practical reasons, colonial American *lingua francas* developed from European languages. Already in parts of Atlantic Africa, *pidgin* languages—pieced together for rudimentary conversation from the mixture of Portuguese or other European languages and various African dialects—had grown along with trading relations. When a *pidgin* blossoms to allow more nuanced forms of expression, and is spoken as a primary language, it becomes a *creole* language. A creole Portuguese called *fala de Guine* developed by the early 16th century and was widely spoken as a trade language along the

African coast. When other Europeans began to trade extensively in Africa, new pidgins and creoles evolved, especially in European trading enclaves.

In the Americas, creole languages flourished. These hybrid languages may have been second or third languages for slaves from Africa, but for their children they were often the mother tongue. As creole languages became the normal means of everyday speech, they came to overshadow "national" languages, even among African-born slaves. At the same time, though, creolized *African* languages also developed in the Americas. For example, the *lingua geral da Mina* (or "general Mina language" of Brazil) came to be spoken by Dahomeans as well as other groups who had been captured in Africa by Dahomeans. And even as Africanized languages gave way to Europeanized ones, linguistic survivals took place, in the form of some phonemes (basic sounds) and verb tenses, as well as certain patterns of verbal or musical interaction, such as "call and response." As late as the 1930s, some North American ex-slaves or their descendants were able to sing in African languages, although they did not understand the words. Historian Michael Gomez argues that refusal to learn or speak standard English was a mark of resistance among North American slaves. In the early 19th-century United States, a large majority of African-born slaves either could not or did not speak recognizable English or French, instead using their native languages with one another, and/or speaking a version of English or French so Africanized as to be unintelligible to whites.

As with languages, African religious practices sometimes persisted in the creole generations, but often were creatively merged with the dominant form of Christianity. New Afro-Christian religions developed, such as Santeria in Cuba, Condomblé in Brazil, Vodou in Haiti, and Afro-Baptist faiths in North America, based on African principles of direct knowledge of and contact with the other world. In Brazil and Cuba, where slaves were supposed to be baptized and non-Christian practices faced legal sanction, new religious traditions were created by grafting Catholic saints onto mostly Yoruba deities like Shango, Ogun, and Osun. Thus the rites and sacrifices associated with these deities became part of the ostensibly Christian worship of the saint with which they were paired. In English-speaking North America, most slaves were not Christians even through the mid-19th century. African Americans, converted or not, participated in spiritual practices of African origin like the ring shout, certain funeral and burial arrangements, and water baptism. And throughout the Americas (as exemplified by the last source in this chapter), African healing techniques based on beliefs about the spiritual world—known variously as voodoo, hoodoo, conjuration, and by other names—persisted, in some ways to the present.

CONCLUSION

From the viewpoint of African and European traders, the men, women, and children who were captured, forcibly marched to the coast, and transported across the Atlantic in the crowded bellies of slave ships were primarily objects of exchange. Their humanity—their need for food, water, and rest, or their vulnerability to illness, their despair, or their yearning to run away or rebel—presented an inconvenience and a threat to profits. Of course, the slave dealers recognized, as well, their prisoners' humanity, for it was New World demand for slaves' human labor power that drove the entire enterprise. But the captives were aliens to the Africans who sold them and racially marked outcasts to the Europeans who bought them; this combined with the desire for material gain suppressed whatever humanitarian feelings might otherwise have been directed to the trade's miserable victims, and shaped the terrible conditions under which they suffered.

Historians do not know how many lives were ended or ruined in the Atlantic slave trade. Perhaps more than 20 million individuals were captured, but only some 12 million survived the land passage to embark on transoceanic ships. In these floating jails, they were crowded into dank and nasty quarters, barely provisioned, and terrorized with violent abuse. Roughly one out of every seven prisoners died. With the sense that they had nothing to lose, nearly all must have been tempted to fight back, and many did—at great risk and usually with horrible consequences for themselves and their comrades. But resistance also probably limited the trade overall, at least hitting captains and slave traders where they could feel it—in the accounting sheet.

Enslaved Africans held onto their humanity not only in their endurance and resistance during the Middle Passage. When they disembarked in the Americas, they brought with them the elements that had made them members of various communities in Africa: their languages, religious practices and beliefs, ideas about kinship and affiliation, and their general manner of doing things. In spite of the violence and alienation of slavery in the New World, and in spite of the necessity of adapting to Africans of other backgrounds and the

European-descended master class, enslaved Africans did not quickly abandon the ways of their homelands. First-generation Africans retained and passed along to their children what pieces they could of the materials and cultures of their places of origin. And even as creolization took place, the American-born continued to be influenced by African languages, musical and dance forms, folk knowledge, and spirituality; and African-derived beads, wood carvings, musical instruments, bottle trees, grave goods, and more were part of their material worlds. Today, the legacy of enslaved Africans lives on in every region of the Americas, where they and their descendants built communities and cultures out of the old and the new.

SOURCES

■ The Coffle to the Coast

Venture Smith, author of the first North American slave narrative, was captured and enslaved as a child somewhere in the hinterland of the Gold Coast. After serving several masters in colonial New England, Venture purchased his freedom in 1765, at the age of 36, and spent his later life with his family in Connecticut. His narrative, dictated to a local schoolteacher, was published in 1798.

After witnessing the murder of his father, a chief, Smith was enslaved by members of a rival army. This selection from his account includes marching in a coffle toward the coast. As you read it, consider the many physical and emotional traumas the boy must have suffered. What were some of his observations? What does he seem to recall most vividly?

The army of the enemy was large, I should suppose consisting of about six thousand men. Their leader was called Baukurre. After destroying the old prince [his father], they decamped and immediately marched towards the sea, lying to the west, taking with them myself and the women prisoners. In the march a scouting party was detached from the main army. To the leader of this party I was made waiter, having to carry his gun, &c. . . . The enemy had remarkable success in destroying the country wherever they went. For as far as they had penetrated, they laid the habitations waste and captured the people. The distance they had now brought me was about four hundred miles. All the march I had very hard tasks imposed on me, which I must perform on pain of punishment. I was obliged to carry on my head a large flat stone used for grinding our corn, weighing as I should suppose, as much as 25 pounds; besides victuals, mat and cooking utensils. Though I was pretty large and stout of my age, yet these burdens were very grievous to me, being only about six years and an half old.

. . . Having come to the next tribe, the enemy laid siege and immediately took men, women, children, flocks, and all their valuable effects. They then went on to the next district which was contiguous to

---

Source: The Narrative of Venture Smith, 1798. *A Narrative of the Life and Adventures of Venture, a Native of Africa, but Resident Above Sixty Years in the United States of America. Related by Himself.* New London: Printed in 1798. Reprinted in AD 1835, and published by a Descendant of Venture. Revised and Republished in 1896 (Middletown, CT: J. S. Stewart, 1897), pp. 10–12.

the sea, called in Africa, Anamaboo. . . . All of us were then put into the castle, and kept for market. On a certain time I and other prisoners were put on board a canoe, under our master, and rowed away to a vessel belonging to Rhode-Island, commanded by Capt. Collingwood, and the mate Thomas Mumford. While we were going to the vessel, our master told us all to appear to the best possible advantage for sale. I was bought on board by one Robertson Mumford, steward of said vessel, for four gallons of rum, and a piece of calico, and called VENTURE, on account of his having purchased me with his own private venture. Thus I came by my name. All the slaves that were bought for that vessel's cargo, were two hundred and sixty.

■ Slavers versus Slaves in the Middle Passage

Alexander Falconbridge traveled as a surgeon on four British slaving voyages between 1780 and 1787. After meeting the activist Thomas Clarkson (whom the reader will encounter in Chapter 4), he joined the antislavery movement. His influential book, based on his own experiences and observations, described the slave trade from the acquisition of captives along the African coast, through their treatment on slave ships, to their sale in the West Indies. Falconbridge's depiction of the Middle Passage, from which the following excerpt was taken, contains details about the slaves' miserable quarters, scant food, shortages of drinking water, and physical punishments. It also suggests a continual struggle between slavers and slaves, with profits and lives as the stakes.

What are some of the ways African captives asserted their own will even under the debilitating circumstances of slave ships? How did slave ship personnel endeavor to control them? What does Falconbridge want to convey about slaves, slavers, and the slave trade to his readers?

Upon the negroes refusing to take sustenance, I have seen coals of fire, glowing hot, put on a shovel, and placed so near their lips, as to scorch and burn them. And this has been accompanied with threats, of forcing them to swallow the coals, if they any longer persisted in refusing to eat. . . . I have also been credibly informed that a certain captain in the slave trade poured melted lead on such of the negroes as obstinately refused their food.

Source: Alexander Falconbridge, *An Account of the Slave Trade on the Coast of Africa, 1788* (London: J. Phillips, George Yard, Lombard Street), pp. 23, 30, 32.

Exercise being deemed necessary for the preservation of their health, they are sometimes obliged to dance, when the weather will permit their coming on deck. If they go about it reluctantly, or do not move with agility, they are flogged; a person standing by them all the time with a cat-o'-nine-tails in his hand for that purpose.... The poor wretches are frequently compelled to sing also; but when they do so, their songs are generally ... melancholy lamentations of their exile from their native country....

As very few of the negroes can so far brook the loss of their liberty, and the hardships they endure ... they are ever upon the watch to take advantage of the least negligence in their oppressors. Insurrections are frequently the consequence; which are seldom suppressed without much bloodshed. Sometimes these are successful, and the whole ship's company is cut off. They are likewise always ready to seize every opportunity for committing some act of desperation to free themselves from their miserable state; and notwithstanding the restraints under which they are laid, they often succeed....

It frequently happens that the negroes, on being purchased by the Europeans, become raving mad; and many of them die in that state, particularly the women....

■ Runaway Communities: The Great Quilombo of Palmares

Throughout the Americas, some slaves were able to run away and form independent settlements of their own. The largest and longest-lasting maroon community was the Brazilian *quilombo* of Palmares. This network of runaway settlements was established in the backlands of northeastern Brazil in the early 17th century and lasted about a hundred years. In 1694 it was destroyed by a Brazilian military expedition.

The following excerpt comes from a chronicle written in the late 17th century by an unnamed writer and first published in 1876. As you read it, think about why the Dutch and then Portuguese governors were so eager to attack Palmares. Why were so many of their attacks unsuccessful?

Source: Pedro Paulino da Fonseca, "Memoria dos feitos que se deram durante os primeiros annos da guerra com os negros quilombolas dos Palmares, seu destroço e paz aceita em Junho de 1678," *Revista do Instituto Histórico e Geográfico Brasileiro* 39 (1876), Part 1, pp. 293–321, in Robert Edgar Conrad, *Children of God's Fire: A Documentary History of Black Slavery in Brazil* (Princeton: Princeton University Press, 1983), pp. 369–70.

What can you infer from this account about the internal structure of Palmares? How was it governed? How did its people survive?

———————————

. . . . It is widely believed that when blacks were first brought into the captaincies of Brazil they began to live in these Palmares, and it is certain that during the period of Dutch rule their numbers greatly increased.

They called their king Gangasuma (a hybrid term meaning "great lord" composed of the Angolan or Bunda word "ganga" and the Tupí [Indian] word "assú"). This king lived in a royal city which they called Macaco. This was the main city among the other towns or *mocambos*, and it was completely surrounded by a wall of earth and sticks.

The second city was that known as Sucupira. . . . Here lived the Gangasona, the king's brother. Like the latter, all the cities were under the command of rulers and powerful chiefs, who lived in them and governed them.

Sucupira, the war command center where the confederation's defense forces and sentinels were trained, was also fortified, but with stone and wood. Nearly a league in length, it contained within its boundaries three lofty mountains and a river called Cachingi, meaning "an abundance of water."

Before the restoration of Pernambuco from Dutch rule, twenty-five probing expeditions were sent into the area, suffering great losses but failing to uncover the secrets of those brave people. . . .

. . . Francisco Barreto, . . . recovering the captaincy from Dutch rule with the surrender of Recife in January, 1654, immediately undertook a campaign against Palmares, since for him these internal enemies were just as harmful and more barbaric and dreadful than the former. . . .

From March, 1657, to January, 1674 . . . it was for no lack of effort that victory was not achieved, because all the governors until that time more or less dealt with the problem. . . . The army's best fighters, the most experienced leaders of the war against the Dutch, were at once employed for this purpose, with immense effort and suffering, but very little achieved.

The inhabitants of Alagôas, Porto Calvo, and Penedo were constantly under attack, and their houses and plantations robbed by the blacks of Palmares. The blacks killed their cattle and carried away their slaves to enlarge their *quilombos* and increase the number of their defenders, forcing the inhabitants and natives of those towns to engage in fighting at a distance of forty leagues or more, at great cost to their plantations and risk to their own lives, without which the blacks would have become masters of the captaincy because of their huge and ever-increasing numbers.

■ "Conjuration" among African Americans

A house slave born in Kentucky in 1815, Henry Bibb began running away for short periods of time at the age of ten. When he was 22 he escaped to free territory; over the next four years he returned to the South attempting to rescue his family, was recaptured, and escaped on five other occasions before settling in the Detroit area and joining the antislavery movement as a public speaker. He began recounting his life story from a lecture platform and published it in 1849.

In Bibb's childhood, running away and conjuration were both techniques for ameliorating the cruelties of slavery. How was conjuration thought to work? What do you think were its origins? Why did Bibb give up on it?

There is much superstition among the slaves. Many of them believe in what they call "conjuration," tricking, and witchcraft; and some of them pretend to understand the art, and say that by it they can prevent their masters from exercising their will over the slaves. Such are often applied to by others, to give them power to prevent their masters from flogging them. The remedy is most generally some kind of bitter root; they are directed to chew it and spit towards their masters when they are angry with their slaves. At other times they prepare certain kinds of powders, to sprinkle about their masters' dwellings. This is all done for the purpose of defending themselves in some peaceable manner, although I am satisfied that there is no virtue at all in it. I have tried it to perfection when I was a slave at the South. . . .

. . . [T]here was another old slave in that neighborhood, who professed to understand all about conjuration, and I thought I would try his skill. He told me that . . . if I would only pay him a certain amount in cash, that he would tell me how to prevent any person from striking me. After I had paid him his charge, he told me to go to the cow-pen after night, and get some fresh cow manure, and mix it with red pepper and white people's hair, all to be put into a pot over the fire, and scorched until it could be ground into snuff. I was then to sprinkle it about my master's bedroom, in his hat and boots, and it would prevent him from ever abusing me in any way. After I got it all ready prepared, the smallest pinch of it scattered over a room, was enough to make a horse sneeze from the strength of it; but it did no good. . . . The old man had my money, and I was treated no better for it.

Source: Henry Bibb, 1849. *Narrative of the Life and Adventures of Henry Bibb, an American Slave, Written by Himself* (New York: Author, 1849), pp. 25–8.

CHAPTER 4

How Did the Slave Trade End?

A SKEPTICAL QUERY

In 1820, Osei Bonsu, powerful king of the Asante, confronted an emissary from the British Empire with a pointed question. "A long time ago," the African monarch said to Joseph Dupuis, "the great king [of England] liked plenty of trade, more than now; then many ships came, and they bought ivory, gold, and slaves; but now he will not let the ships come as before, and the people buy gold and ivory only. This is what I have in my head, so now tell me truly, like a friend, why does the king do so?"

Osie Bonsu had good reason to wonder. Twelve years before, the world's greatest slave-trading nation—whose merchants shipped nearly 30,000 Africans to the Americas per year by the end of the 18th century, and whose West Indian colonies generated massive profits by slave labor—had abolished its slave trade. By the time the Asante king conversed with Dupuis, British officials were working to extend the ban on slave trafficking to other Europeans and Africans as well. Within another 20 years they would abolish slavery itself in Britain's colonies, preceding mainland North American slave emancipation by three decades. Yet given that people all over the world had accepted slavery as a legitimate institution for thousands of years, and Britons were profiting handsomely from it, what accounts for the United Kingdom's dramatic reversal?

PROFITS AND THE SLAVE TRADE

"What a glorious and advantageous trade this is," wrote an employee in a firm of British slave merchants in 1725. "It is the hinge on which all the trade of this globe moves." Twenty years later the British pamphleteer Malachy Postlethwayt asserted that "the Negroe-Trade and the natural consequences resulting from it may be justly esteemed an inexhaustible fund of wealth and naval power to this nation." The slave trade, he wrote, was "the first principle and foundation of all the rest, the mainspring of the machine which sets every wheel in motion." Indeed, slave-driven economies were thriving in the 18th century, offering little economic incentive for abolishing the African trade. The British Empire's greatest wealth lay in its West Indian colonies, completely dependent on slave labor, which accounted for more than 30 percent of British imports at the turn of the 19th century.

In addition to making the entire system of New World slavery possible, the slave trade itself also brought great fortunes to the merchants and financiers involved in it. Historians have calculated that on average, slave-trading voyages yielded profits of about 10 percent to investors, compared to annual returns of 3.5 percent for British government bonds, 4.5 percent for real estate mortgages, and 6–11 percent for investments in West Indian plantations. Investment in the French slave trade brought a return of 7–10 percent annually, slightly less than the English trade, although the government offered considerable tax breaks as incentives to French merchants. The most profitable branch of 18th-century slave trafficking was probably that of the Portuguese and Brazilians. Because the Portuguese controlled a sizeable stretch of the Angolan coast, they were able to avoid competition with other Europeans. Their purchasing monopoly also allowed them to institute credit systems that were highly advantageous to the Lisbon merchants who financed the voyages.

Profits of the slave trade accrued beyond the direct investors and personnel, however, especially in the major ports where voyages were outfitted, such as Liverpool, Nantes, Lisbon, or Charleston. Many of these cities' leading families lived on fortunes accumulated at least in part through slave trading. Charleston's Henry Laurens, one of the wealthiest men in colonial America and one-time president of the Continental Congress, was also one of the South's major slave importers. In Liverpool, some 25 of today's street names commemorate the slave-dealing businessmen of two or three centuries ago. Trading houses, banks, merchants, and entrepreneurs all became closely involved in the economic activity dependent on the slave trade, and their profits in turn helped to support a wide range of townspeople, such as shipbuilders, carpenters, bakers, petty traders, shopkeepers, tailors, and so on. One of the largest riots in 18th-century England, for instance, occurred in Liverpool in 1774 when sailors attacked slave ships and turned the ships' guns on the city houses of slave-ship owners. The seamen were not protesting the slave trade, however, but their low wages—or rather, the share of the income they received from the slave trade. According to a Parliamentary report on the Liverpool slave trade in the mid-1790s, "This great annual return of wealth may be said to pervade the whole town, increasing the fortunes of the principal adventurers, and contributing to the support of the majority of the inhabitants. . . ."

IDEOLOGY AND REVOLUTION

In spite of the slave trade's economic importance, new currents in the 18th century led people to begin questioning its legitimacy. Evangelical Christianity, which swept through both Great Britain and its North American colonies, offered an egalitarian God relatively unconcerned with man-made hierarchies. Enlightenment thinking, with some exceptions, stressed individual freedoms and inalienable natural rights—concepts central to the 1776–1848 wave of political revolutions in the Americas and Europe. Even the new scientific study of economics, as exemplified by Adam Smith, cast doubt on the profitability of slave labor. Earlier there had been a few abolitionist thinkers and people who saw the slave trade as immoral, but theirs were isolated voices with no serious impact on European ideology. But in the late 18th century influential individuals began to view slavery as antithetical to a modern market economy, or considered it a fundamental challenge to the newly emerging concept of the equality of all men, or held it to be basically anti-Christian.

The American War of Independence, which was profoundly influenced by these new ways of thinking, challenged both the ideology and practice of slavery. As white Americans revolted against what they often called British colonial "slavery," many were forced to confront the contradiction of owning slaves themselves (as the first source at the end of this chapter illustrates). For instance, the slave Prince, who accompanied his master Captain William Whipple and was one of the oarsmen who rowed George Washington across the Delaware River in 1776, reportedly told Whipple, "Master, *you* are going to fight for your *liberty,* but I have none to fight for." Whipple at this point realized that he could no longer keep Prince as a slave. In *The Watchman's Alarm* (1774), popular Baptist preacher and pamphleteer John Allen questioned the values of his fellow colonists who compared colonization to slavery, asking rhetorically, "What is a trifling three-penny duty on tea compared to inestimable blessings of liberty to one captive?"

Meanwhile, slaves and free black people turned revolutionary rhetoric and the ideology of freedom against the institution of American slavery, essentially echoing the British writer Samuel Johnson's wry query: "How is it that we hear the loudest yelps for liberty among the drivers of negroes?" As early as 1765, slaves in Charleston, South Carolina, watched white protesters against the Stamp Act marching and chanting, "Liberty! Liberty! And stamp'd paper." Before long a group of the city's slaves also began shouting, "Liberty! Liberty!"—provoking some panic among Charleston's whites. Several times in the early 1770s, free and enslaved African Americans in New England petitioned the legislature for emancipation and cited their natural rights, in one case appealing to "the divine spirit of *freedom* [that] seems to fire every human breast on this continent."

Further, the massive disruption caused by the Revolutionary War offered opportunities for slaves to escape their masters, on such an enormous scale that historians now recognize the Revolution as the largest slave revolt in U.S. history. Some of the fugitives joined the fighting forces, although leaders on both sides were wary of alienating important slaveholders and fomenting slave insurrection. Although African American soldiers had fought side by side with whites at the battles of Lexington, Concord, and Bunker Hill, George Washington barred their further recruitment when he took command of the Continental Army in 1775. By 1777, however, manpower was in short supply, and leaders in various northern towns and states began to recruit black soldiers. Two years later the Continental Congress even voted to enlist and arm some 3,000 slave troops in South Carolina and Georgia, although the plan was never enacted. Altogether about 5,000 African Americans enlisted in the Continental Army, and hundreds more served at sea.

More ex-slaves fought for the Crown, however. The Governor of Virginia, whose royal title was Lord Dunmore, sought to disrupt the American cause by promising freedom to any slaves who would desert Patriot masters and join the Loyalist forces (although runaway slaves belonging to Loyalists were returned to their masters). Dunmore officially issued his proclamation in November, 1775, and within a month 300 black men had joined his "Ethiopian Regiment." Probably no more than 800 eventually succeeded in joining Dunmore's ranks, but his proclamation inspired thousands of runaways to follow behind British lines throughout the war. Later, a 1779 proclamation by Sir Henry Clinton at Philipsburg, New York, vaguely suggested that slaves who deserted the rebels and joined his forces would be protected from re-enslavement; and as his troops moved through the South, thousands more slaves escaped. Between 4,000 and 5,000 bedraggled African Americans, including 30 of Thomas Jefferson's slaves, followed General Cornwallis's army across Virginia to Yorktown. Altogether, the British invasion, occupation, and final withdrawal from the southern states reduced the ranks of slaves by some 100,000.

Many of the fugitives who cast their lot with the Tories were motivated by the news that slavery had been outlawed in Britain. In a 1772 case involving a Virginia slave named James Somerset, who ran away while in England with his master, Britain's High Court had ruled that slavery would not be enforced on English soil. One American escapee so closely linked England and liberty that he renamed himself "British Freedom." But at the end of the war, British officials disappointed ex-slaves who looked to them for protection. Although British ships evacuated thousands of African American fugitives, they left behind many more to face recapture. Some of the evacuees ended up as slaves in the Bahamas; thousands of others, including the veterans of some black military units, were enslaved in the British West Indies. Some 1,200 African American refugees soon comprised the "black poor" of London. British officials shipped the largest group of freed slaves to Nova Scotia, where they suffered harsh conditions, poor soil, and the disdain of the local white population. Eventually, over 1,000 of these Canadian blacks were shipped to the tiny British abolitionist colony at Sierra Leone (which is discussed later).

Back in North America, African Americans' demands for liberty forced white revolutionary leaders to struggle with slavery as a policy issue. The first drafts of two key documents of U.S. history, the Declaration of Independence and the Constitution, both originally contained clauses opposing slave-trading (in the case of the Constitution, outlawing it), until delegates from South Carolina and Georgia had the clauses removed from each. In April 1776, representatives of the 13 rebellious colonies meeting in the Continental Congress voted to halt the slave trade, more out of a desire to harm British trade than opposition to slavery. Three months later, the Continental Congress grappled with slavery again. In his first version of the Declaration of Independence, Thomas Jefferson wrote a scathing indictment of King George for promoting slavery in the New World: "[King George] has waged cruel war on human nature itself, violating its most sacred rights of life and liberty in the persons of a distant people who never offended him, captivating and carrying them into slavery in another hemisphere, or to incur miserable death in their transportation thither." As delegates collectively edited the document, this passage was removed. The Declaration of Independence became the world's foremost manifesto celebrating human rights and personal freedom, yet at the time it was written, its author Thomas Jefferson owned over 200 slaves.

The American Revolution's effects on slavery were similarly contradictory. On one hand, the number of free African Americans increased dramatically. Northern states, like the United Kingdom, became places with "free soil." Between the beginning of the war and the early 19th century, every northern state enacted some plan of emancipation. The North's free black population swelled from several hundred in the 1770s to over 150,000 by 1810, while slavery contracted. Even in the South, there were increasing numbers of freed people, mostly because so many liberated themselves. By the end of the Revolutionary War, one-third of Georgia's slaves had become free, and the black population of South Carolina declined by about 25 percent.

But slavery also became firmly entrenched in the United States. At the Constitutional Convention of 1787, southern delegates forced several compromises that protected bondage in a new nation that espoused liberty. For the purposes of taxation and congressional representation, each slave counted as three-fifths of a free person— a system that supported the political power of slaveholders and denigrated the humanity of the enslaved. The Fugitive Slave Clause affirmed the rights of slaveholders to reclaim runaways who escaped beyond the borders of slave states. And Southerners won a constitutional guarantee that the Atlantic slave trade could continue without federal interference for the next 20 years. Georgia resumed slave imports from Africa until 1798, when the Haitian Revolution brought fears of creating too dense a slave population; South Carolina brought in some 38,000 African slaves between its reopening of the trade in 1803 and final abolition in 1808.

ANTISLAVERY IN THE UNITED KINGDOM

In the early United States, the importance national leaders placed on political unity essentially allowed Southern interests to derail the Northern-based antislavery movement. In Britain, however, the American war was fortuitous for abolitionists, not only because it helped to popularize ideas about individual liberty, but also because proslavery advocates from the American South no longer had influence in the British Empire. Already British Quakers, along with their American counterparts, had begun to see slavery as immoral. From the 1750s, the 90,000 English-speaking Quakers on both sides of the Atlantic had started urging members to abandon both slave ownership and participation in the slave trade. In 1775, Quakers founded the Pennsylvania Abolition Society, the first such organization in North America. It was reorganized in 1787 as the Pennsylvania Society for Promoting the Abolition of Slavery, the Relief of Free Negroes Unlawfully Held in Bondage, and for Improving the Condition of the African Race (Benjamin Franklin later became its president). Similar organizations were founded in 11 other states.

British Quakers, responding to their Pennsylvania brethren, established the first British antislavery society in 1783, the year peace with the colonies was achieved. As a religious minority vulnerable to persecution, Quakers already had considerable experience in political lobbying as well as an established national network of regional and local groups on which they could rely for support. In 1787, the original members of the Quaker committee joined together with a number of non-Quakers—including Granville Sharp, an Evangelical Anglican lawyer who had successfully argued the Somerset decision before Britain's High Court—to form the Society for the Abolition of the Slave Trade. Thomas Clarkson, who had written a prize-winning essay attacking slavery as a student at Cambridge University, became the organization's full-time agent, traveling thousands of miles on horseback to gather information and organize support throughout the country. William Wilberforce, a wealthy philanthropist and Member of Parliament, became the movement's principal parliamentary spokesman.

Although the reformers opposed slavery itself, they saw the Atlantic slave trade as the worst part of the institution and the easiest piece to attack. They made the tactical decision to concentrate on abolishing the trade, hoping and assuming that slave-owners would treat their slaves better if there were no source of new slaves, and that the end of the slave trade would ultimately lead to the abolition of slavery. The members of the Abolition Committee also took up two initial tasks. First, they created an organization encompassing a central London-based national committee and its parliamentary spokesmen, who were responsible for formulating policy and coordinating action, along with satellite affiliates throughout the country. These auxiliary antislavery societies ranged from large, well-funded organizations in cities like Manchester and Bristol to local church groups elsewhere. At the same time, Clarkson and others began gathering and publishing a number of shocking accounts of the slave trade, which—together with revelations about the high death rate among white sailors in the trade—were intended to turn public and parliamentary opinion against it.

Some of this material came from people with direct experience in the slave trade. John Newton, a former slave ship captain who had experienced a dramatic religious conversion and repudiated his earlier life (and who wrote the hymn "Amazing Grace") published *Thoughts upon the African Slave Trade* in 1788. The same year, Alexander Falconbridge, a former doctor on a slave ship, published *An Account of the Slave Trade on the Coast of Africa* (one of the sources in Chapter 3). But equally if not more important to the antislavery campaign was the testimony of African ex-slaves, notably Olaudah Equiano and Ottobah Cugoano. According to his own account, Equiano was kidnapped inland from the Bight of Biafra when he was about ten years old.[1] His peripatetic childhood in slavery was spent in Virginia, the West Indies, England, and at sea as the servant of a naval officer. He became free in the 1760s at about the age of 21, and in the 1770s in London he became a devout Methodist. In the early 1780s, Equiano emerged as a leader of London's African community and an antislavery activist. Along with his friend Cugoano, Equiano helped Granville Sharp publicize the terrible facts of the *Zong* case, in which (as mentioned in Chapter 3) the owner of a slave ship attempted to collect insurance for 133 African slaves whom the captain had ordered thrown overboard. Ottobah Cugoano, an ex-slave from the Gold Coast, published his *Thoughts and Sentiments on the Evils of Slavery* in 1787, denouncing the "abominable, mean, beastly, cruel, bloody slavery carried on by the inhuman, barbarous Europeans against the poor unfortunate Black Africans," and describing slavery as "an injury and robbery contrary to all law, civilization, reason, justice, equity, and charity." The book was rapidly translated into French and appeared in Paris the following year. In 1789, the publication of Equiano's memoir created an even bigger sensation. *The Interesting Narrative of the Life of Olaudah Equiano, or Gustavus Vassa* went into nine British editions in his lifetime and ten posthumously, while unauthorized editions and translations appeared in Holland (1790), New York (1791), Germany (1792), and Russia (1794). For years Equiano traveled almost incessantly to speak and sell his book in the major towns of the United Kingdom.

Using their extensive nationwide organization and gripping accounts of the slave trade, the London and other British abolition societies pursued three inter-related strategies. First, abolitionists organized mass meetings, through their own societies or through churches, throughout the United Kingdom. At such events, activists regaled their audiences with the horrors of the Atlantic slave trade, sometimes showing its gruesome hardware—like manacles, chains, and devices for prying open slaves' mouths—to amplify the audience's outrage. The meetings inevitably ended with a call for

---

[1]See footnote 1 of Chapter 1 on the controversy about Equiano's origins.

contributions to help fund the movement and with the circulation of petitions intended for Parliament, the abolitionists' second major tactic. Although Members of Parliament were elected by a very limited segment of the population (and the House of Lords was not elected at all), they still could be swayed by public opinion. The central antislavery society launched its first mass petition campaign in 1787–88, generating a tremendous response. In Manchester alone, nearly 11,000 men signed antislavery petitions, representing some two-thirds of the city's adult male population. Although women were not solicited for signatures, they constituted 10 percent of the contributors to the national campaign. In all, Parliament received about a hundred petitions containing perhaps 60,000 names. Subsequent petition drives were even larger: in 1792, the government received 519 antislave trade or antislavery petitions, containing some 390,000 signatures. Beginning in 1791, antislavery supporters unleashed their third major weapon, a boycott of slave-produced products, especially sugar. Pamphlets with titles like *An Address to the People of Great Britain, on the Propriety of Abstaining from West India Sugar and Rum* sold in the tens of thousands. Clarkson estimated that at least 300,000 people gave up sugar; in several parts of the country, grocers reported sugar sales dropping by 33 to 50 percent over just a few months. In all of these actions—mass meetings, lobbying lawmaking bodies, and boycotts—antislavery protesters of the late 18th century pioneered tactics still used by advocates for social change today.

Even in the era before photography, visual imagery formed a key element in the antislavery campaign. As early as 1787, members of the London Abolition Society designed the now well-known depiction of a black man in chains, later reproduced at Josiah Wedgewood's renowned pottery factory, with the caption "Am I Not a Man and a Brother?" (Figure 4.1). In 1788, a consignment of the cameos was shipped to Benjamin Franklin in Philadelphia, where the medallions became a fashion statement for abolitionists and antislavery sympathizers. They were worn as bracelets and hair ornaments, and even inlaid with gold as decoration for snuffboxes. Soon the fashion extended to the general public, who saw the image not only on jewelry but also on the covers of antislavery publications. But the most potent image in the movement's arsenal was a diagram Clarkson managed to secure, of a fully loaded slave ship, the *Brooks,* with top, side, and end views of 482 slaves closely lined up in rows

FIGURE 4.1 "Am I Not a Man and a Brother?" Created in 1787, and reproduced by Josiah Wedgwood, this kneeling figure became the central icon of the antislavery movement. What elements do you think made it such a powerful and effective image?

(Figure 4.2). The illustration of the *Brooks* appeared in newspapers, magazines, books, and pamphlets; the Antislavery Society printed more than 7,000 copies of it on posters, which were hung on walls throughout the country. Clarkson wrote that the diagram, these days reproduced in nearly every publication dealing with the slave trade, "seemed to make an instantaneous impression of horror upon all who saw it."

Amidst this popular organizing, Wilberforce and his allies introduced antislave trade legislation in Parliament beginning in 1789. At his instigation, a Select Committee of the House of Commons examined witnesses and evidence on the slave trade in 1790 and 1791. In 1792, Wilberforce actually persuaded the House of Commons to outlaw the slave trade in four years' time, although the bill was delayed to death in

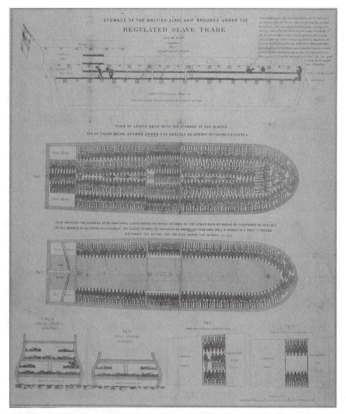

FIGURE 4.2   Diagram of the slave ship *Brooks,* illustrating how captives were crammed inside. This 1788 illustration was an important piece of evidence for the abolitionist movement.

the more conservative House of Lords. But beginning in 1793, activists in Britain were confronted with a major obstacle to abolition: war with France and, somewhat paradoxically, the self-emancipation of half a million slaves in St. Domingue.

REVOLUTION IN ST. DOMINGUE

The Haitian Revolution began as a rebellion against slavery and French plantation owners in the context of the French Revolution, but it lasted for 13 years and resulted in St. Domingue's independence from France. By 1804 the revolution had destroyed the dominant white population, the plantation system, and the institution of slavery in the most prosperous colony in the Americas, which then became the world's first independent black republic. The revolution in St. Domingue inspired enslaved people throughout the Americas to press for freedom and fueled abolitionists' arguments that slaves could achieve greatness and that cataclysm was inevitable unless slavery was overturned. Like the American Revolution, however, it also buttressed slavery, in part by convincing some whites in diverse locations that slaves were savages and had to be controlled ever more tightly. In the United Kingdom, the abolition movement made little progress while St. Domingue's slaves were in bloody revolt.

As mentioned in Chapter 1, by the late 1700s, the French colony of St. Domingue had developed into the richest European colony in the Western Hemisphere. With thousands of sugar and coffee plantations based on African slave labor, St. Domingue exported more than all of the British North American colonies combined. At the pinnacle of its social and economic system were approximately 40,000 white colonists, including about 10,000 plantation-owning aristocrats (*grands blancs*) and a middle class of about 30,000 shopkeepers, artisans, soldiers, and others (*petit blancs*). Some 28,000 free people of color (*gens de couleur*) were mostly small planters or urban merchants, many of whom owned slaves. While this group aspired to the status of the white elite, its members faced discrimination because of their racial background. In turn, they had little sympathy for the nearly half-million slaves from Africa or of African descent, who were worked so brutally and relentlessly that constant importations barely kept pace with the outlandish death rate.

The outbreak of the French Revolution in 1789 dramatically destabilized the wealthy French slave colony. Elite planters sent a delegation to the new Estates-General in Paris to seek more self-government and greater economic freedom from the metropole. The *gens de couleur* also sent representatives to press for an end to racial discrimination and some political equality with whites. As the French Revolution became more radical, the *gens de couleur* forged an alliance with sympathetic French revolutionaries, who identified the wealthy planters on the island as royalists. In 1791, the government in France decreed that persons of color whose parents were free should be entitled to vote. St. Domingue's white inhabitants refused to implement the decree, however, and free people of color took up arms to demand their rights. When Vincent Ogé, the leader of the *gens de couleur* mission in France, returned to organize an army, planter forces captured and executed him, along with several hundred others. By this point the island's whites, led by the planters, and the *gens de couleur* were engaged in open warfare. Both sides armed their slaves.

The division between the two groups of slave-owners gave slaves an opening. There had been small-scale revolts before, and groups of maroons already lived on the island. When a (false) rumor circulated that French troops were coming to oppose the planters, slaves in the northern part of the colony rebelled. Within a month, at least 40,000 and maybe as many as 100,000 slaves joined the revolt. Plantations were destroyed, masters and overseers were killed, and crops burned. Accounts of the rebellion describe widespread torching of property, fields, factories, and anything else that belonged to, or served, slaveholders. The inferno is said to have burned almost continuously for months. Soldiers sent from France to quell the rebellion arrived slowly and died rapidly in fever epidemics. The ex-slaves fell in large numbers to the colonists' firepower and were forced to withdraw, but many scattered bands kept fighting. The initial rebellion left an estimated 10,000 blacks and 2,000 whites dead and more than 1,000 plantations sacked and razed.

By the end of 1792, the slave uprising had become a full-scale civil war, as whites, free people of color, and former slaves all fought for their own interests, with shifting alliances and mutual hatred. At one time, as many as six warring factions were in the field simultaneously: slaves, free people of color, two classes of whites (*petits blancs* and *grands blancs*), and invading Spanish and English troops—each attempting to capitalize on the French loss of control—as well as the French forces trying to restore their authority. In the midst of this whirlwind, Francois Dominique Toussaint L'Ouverture, described by a contemporary French general as "a black Spartacus," emerged as the most formidable military and political leader. A literate ex-slave and ex-slave owner, Toussaint took part in the slave revolt and, with other black rebel leaders, joined forces with the Spanish army in the north against the French. A brilliant tactician who could appeal to both Africans and island-born blacks, Toussaint rose to high rank within the Spanish army. Then in 1793, after French revolutionary officials abolished slavery in an attempt to gain black allies and defeat the white elite, he switched sides. By 1795 Toussaint had been promoted to general by French colonial officials, and he drove out the Spanish forces. In 1797, Toussaint became governor-general of the colony, and over the next four years he expelled all invading forces and created a new constitution. His army, composed mainly of former slaves, at times numbered more than 20,000 men. Toussaint negotiated the final withdrawal of British troops from the island and, sidestepping the French Republic's official policies (for France was at war with Britain), secured favorable commercial and political arrangements with Britain and the United States. Despite orders from Paris, his troops occupied Spanish Santo Domingo (which shared the island of Hispañola with St. Domingue), and in 1801 Toussaint declared himself governor-general for life.

Toussant L'Ouverture's rise to power in St. Domingue came as an affront to Napoleon Bonaparte, now head of state in France. Although Toussaint continued to assert his loyalty to France, he left the French government no effective role in local affairs. Napoleon sought to return St. Domingue to French control and, to restore the colony's former prosperity, reinstate slavery. In 1802, Napoleon sent 16,000 troops (later increased to 30,000) under the command of his brother-in-law, Charles Leclerc, to subjugate St. Domingue. Thousands succumbed to the ex-slave guerrilla forces as well as to malaria and yellow fever (which killed Leclerc). But the French forces wore away at rebel resistance. Tricked into negotiating a deceptive French surrender, Toussaint was captured and sent to France, where he died in a freezing mountain fortress.

The news that slavery had been reintroduced in Guadeloupe and Martinique, however, along with outrage at the French treachery, provoked another popular uprising. This new revolt was led by two of Toussaint's ex-slave subordinates, Jean Jacques Dessalines and Henri Christophe, in alliance with the leader of the free people of color Alexandre Pétion. Few women had taken up arms during the first stages of the revolution, but now large numbers of women actively supported the resistance. In this gruesome period, the revolution turned into a race war, as the French determined to exterminate most of the existing African-descended population, who could, they calculated, later be replaced by new slaves. Each side terrorized the other with massacres and brutality. By the end of the war, St. Domingue's population had been reduced by more than half. But assisted by disease and a British naval blockade, the rebels forced the French to evacuate St. Domingue in late 1803. In less than two years the French had lost 40,000 men to wounds and yellow fever; by 1805 nearly all the other whites had been massacred or driven off the island. On January 1, 1804, Dessalines declared himself emperor and proclaimed the independence of Haiti, changing the country's name to the Arawak word for "high land."

Although Haiti continued to be plagued by violence and poverty, its very existence challenged every slaveholding society in the New

World. For the first time, whites saw a massive, invincible slave revolt, and blacks saw that it was possible to win the fight for freedom. News of the revolution spread widely and rapidly, carried in part by the thousands of white and black refugees who fanned out from St. Domingue throughout the Atlantic world. Within one month of the 1791 slave uprising, slaves in Jamaica were singing songs about it. Over the next few years, slave-owners from Virginia and Louisiana to Cuba and Brazil complained of a new "insolence" on the part of their slaves, which they attributed to awareness of the successful slave revolution. Even in distant Rio de Janeiro, some free black and mixed-race militiamen were found in 1805 to be wearing around their necks medallion portraits of the emperor Dessalines, who had been crowned only months before. Slave revolts and conspiracies in the Caribbean averaged at least two per year between 1789 and 1817 and nearly four per year in the 1790s. There and in mainland North America, slave conspirators had ideological and personal connections to Haiti. In Louisiana in 1811, the transplanted Haitian Charles Deslondes led the largest slave revolt in North American history. In 1822 Denmark Vesey, who had briefly lived in St. Domingue, promised his followers the help of Haitian soldiers once they had taken over the city of Charleston. As Frederick Douglass reminded his audience at the 1893 Columbian Exposition in Chicago, "the freedom you and I enjoy to-day; . . . the freedom that eight hundred thousand colored people enjoy in the British West Indies; the freedom that has come to the colored race the world over, is largely due to the brave stand taken by the black sons of Haiti. . . . When they struck for freedom . . . they struck for the freedom of every black man in the world."

But paradoxically, the Haitian Revolution also resulted in an expansion of slavery and a hardening of anti-abolition ideologies. In the absence of competition from St. Domingue, planters in the Spanish West Indies revitalized slave-based agricultural production, expanding the Atlantic slave trade to Cuba in particular. The French failure to regain control over St. Domingue also influenced Napoleon to abandon efforts to build an empire in the Western Hemisphere. In 1803, France sold its North American province of Louisiana, a region of more than 800,000 square miles, to the United States. With the newly invented cotton gin fueling the expansion of commercial agriculture, the Deep South soon became the epicenter of North American slavery. And just as Haiti's example inspired slave resistance and abolitionist sentiments, it also horrified proslavery whites. Fixating on news of the massacres that preceded Haitian independence, many became convinced that freeing slaves would result in massive violence against white people, and they became even less willing than before to end slavery peacefully.

Combined with news of violent upheaval in France, the St. Domingue Revolution helped to stall the abolition movement in Britain in the 1790s. In a 1793 Parliamentary speech, for instance, the Earl of Abingdon rose to attack the antislavery movement, crying, "What are the rights of man, but the foolish principles of this new philosophy? If proofs are wanting, look at the colony of St. Domingue and see what the rights of man have done here." Parliament, composed largely of nervous aristocrats, feared the lower-class abolition societies, ridiculing them as "English Jacobins." When in the 1790s the French government allied with Toussaint's armies, the British even found themselves in the position of fighting in the Caribbean to restore slavery. The legacy of Haiti and France haunted Britain for years, as Parliament voted down abolitionist proposals in 1797, 1798, 1799, and 1802.

FINAL SLAVE TRADE ABOLITION

Although much of the British public had turned against slavery and the slave trade by the end of the 18th century, it was not until the international context shifted that abolitionists scored decisive legislative victories. After Britain's enemy France fought to restore slavery in Haiti and then in 1804 resumed the slave trade to its remaining colonies, the final abolition bills were pushed through Parliament under the cloak of English patriotism. Abolitionists shrewdly decided to focus on the British slave trade to *foreign* colonies—a large percentage of the total British commerce—with the justification that such trade would only help develop Britain's current or future international rivals. After Prime Minister Pitt forbade the importation of slaves from Africa into colonies which Britain had captured in the war with France (such as Trinidad), abolitionists were able to push through Parliament a bill prohibiting British slave trading to *all* foreign nations. This eliminated the majority of Britain's slave trade, leading the way for passage in 1807 of a total ban on the British slave trade. British participation in the Atlantic slave trade ended on the first day of 1808, the same date a similar prohibition came into effect in the United States.

Antislavery activists in the United Kingdom realized, however, that traders from other nations would continue to ship slaves from Africa to the Americas, and in fact would expand their operations as

Britons withdrew. So the British antislavery committees, now numbering more than a thousand, pressed the British government to use its international influence and force other nations to stop the trade, as well as to abolish slavery completely in Britain's colonies. As the Napoleonic Wars came to an end in 1814–15, abolitionists collected some 750,000 signatures on 800 petitions demanding that England force France and other European nations to abolish their slave trades. Although the Congress of Vienna issued only an abstract condemnation of slave trafficking, British diplomats did secure treaties by which France and other major continental powers agreed to abolish their slave trades, with Portugal agreeing to end slave trading north of the equator (which, of course, included neither Brazil nor Angola). The Spanish government tried to placate British demands while it procrastinated as long as possible. It did sign a treaty in 1817 abolishing its trade north of the equator and allowing British officials to search Spanish vessels, and in 1820 it promised total abolition of the Spanish slave trade. But these treaties were only slowly put into practice, while Cuban planters continued to import slaves from Africa. Similarly in Brazil, which became independent from Portugal in 1822, officials disagreed with concessions made by Portugal and demanded that the trade south of the equator continue. In 1830, convinced by promises of British economic aid, Brazil's leaders prohibited its African slave trade, although like Spain's officials, they allowed the illegal slave trade to continue.

Even without the participation of Britain, formerly Europe's largest slave-trading nation, human commerce across the Atlantic persisted. Between 3 and 4 million enslaved people were shipped from Africa in the 19th century, accounting for roughly a third of the trade's total volume. From the peak years of the 1780s, when close to 80,000 slaves per year were crossing the Atlantic to the Americas, the trade was only down to about 60,000 per year by the 1820s. After 1830, when the African slave trade became illegal in most places, its volume declined to 43,000 per year in the 1840s. The elimination of Brazil as a market after 1850 dropped the volume to 14,000 per year, and by the early 1860s, the rate was less than 4,000 per year. It declined slowly largely because the illegal trade was highly lucrative to the slave traders and ship-owners who were involved in it. Nor was it confined to one or two nations. Capital, ships, and sailors from a variety of countries, including Britain, the United States, Cuba, Brazil, Spain, and Portugal, flowed into the Atlantic slave trade until its termination. According to one estimate, at least 90 percent of the manufactured goods used in the 19th-century transatlantic slave trade to Brazil and Cuba actually came from Britain, and British credit financed half of the Cuban and Brazilian slave trade.

Still, the British government backed its diplomatic efforts with direct antislave trade interventions. In 1819, British lawmakers established a naval squadron to intercept slave ships, which was stationed off the African coast until the end of the century. The United States and France ultimately set up small antislave trade squadrons as well. Later, treaty agreements as well as unilateral British legislation authorized the British Navy to stop and search ships suspected of carrying slaves, and to seize and condemn any ships equipped for the slave trade on either side of the Atlantic. The fates of such ships, and the roughly 160,000 slaves carried within them, were determined by so-called "courts of mixed commission," comprised of British and other nations' officials and located at various sites in Africa and the Americas. Such courts released thousands of captives to face uncertain futures in Havana, Rio de Janeiro, and St. Helena (an island in the South Atlantic). But the most important site where British personnel settled ex-captives was on the African coast, at Sierra Leone.

Already before 1819, when the first commission was established at Freetown, abolitionists had looked to Sierra Leone as an answer to the "problem" of Britain's black population. At the same time as the Abolition Society was being founded in London, Granville Sharp hatched a scheme to resettle some of the black people there, many poor and in legal trouble, on the coast of Africa. The "black poor" of London could be transformed into a flourishing, free agricultural community, he reasoned, an example of the way things could be without the slave trade. At that time there were more than 1,200 free people of African descent in London, and at least 14,000 in England. The government agreed to ship them out, and a first settlement was established in 1787 at Freetown, Sierra Leone. The colony began with an estimated population of 341 black men, 70 white women prostitutes, and a handful of white Englishmen. The venture was a disaster: some of the settlers were re-enslaved, some turned slavers, many died, and in 1789 quarrels with local inhabitants led a neighboring ruler to burn down the settlement.

Sharp and other prominent abolitionists then sought new settlers, this time from Canada. As mentioned already, during the American

Revolution the British had helped free tens of thousands of American slaves, transporting some to Nova Scotia and others to England itself (and leaving many others to be re-enslaved in the United States). The resettled ex-slaves in Nova Scotia were given the poorest land on the barren Atlantic coast, and by 1791, many were facing famine. The next year the British government chartered 16 ships to bring a thousand former American slaves from Nova Scotia to Sierra Leone. John Clarkson, the brother of the abolitionist Thomas Clarkson, led the project. Later, some 550 deported Jamaican maroons were landed there. The small colony was never self-sufficient, though, and many settlers abandoned Freetown.

Sierra Leone's fortunes changed with the abolition of slave trade. As of January 1, 1808, when its population numbered about 2,000, it became a crown colony. British officials decided that Sierra Leone should be the relocation destination for slaves freed by British naval squadrons off the African coast, regardless of these slaves' origins, and regardless of the opinions of Africans who already lived there. By 1814 there were 10,000 "recaptives" (i.e., people rescued from slave ships) in the colony, mostly in Freetown. Over the next half century, about 3,000 new recaptives were landed at Sierra Leone per year, eventually numbering more than 150,000. Speaking over 120 separate languages, they grouped in communities like "Congo Town," based on their geographic origins. Missionaries and other reformers set up churches and schools for the recaptives, hoping to promote through them Christianity and Western culture in Africa. With their familiarity with the English language, mission Christianity, and Western education, recaptives and their descendents created a new Anglo-African society. Over time, they influenced other Africans both in the vicinity of Freetown and as far away as the Bight of Benin, where thousands of Yoruba-speaking "Saro" (as Sierra Leonians in Nigeria were called) migrated in the middle decades of the 19th century.

Besides the naval patrols, other British abolition efforts focused on ending the slave trade from the supply side. As suggested in Chapter 2, African merchants and rulers had become enmeshed in a slave-supplying system which brought many of them wealth and power. In fact, there were probably more slaves in Africa in 1808 than there were in the Americas. African leaders like Osei Bonsu were justifiably skeptical that their largest slave-trading partner had now turned against this lucrative commerce. Yet as the external demand for captives slowly declined, African elites revived old trades or developed new exports so as to maintain their access to European imports. On the Gold Coast, for example, annual exports of gold climbed to nearly 25,000 ounces in the 1840s and 1850s, compared to 10,000 ounces in the 1790s. During the first half of the 19th century a range of West African commodities supplanted the export of captives, most significantly palm products and groundnuts (both of which yielded oil used as lubricants in industrial machinery) from the Bights of Benin and Biafra and from Senegambia. Reformers particularly from Britain supported such "legitimate trade," along with missionary attempts to spread Christianity, as efforts to atone for the slave trade and redeem what they increasingly saw as "savage" Africa.

The transatlantic slave trade ended for good after international pressure brought its effective prohibition in Brazil and Cuba. In 1850 the British Navy blockaded Brazilian ports, a move that was technically illegal, although there was no public defense of slave trading either within Brazil or internationally. A Brazilian law of the same year outlawed slave importation from Africa and was effectively enforced by Brazilian and British authorities. Spanish Cuba ended its slave trade in 1866, after a treaty and naval action involving both Britain and the United States. With the end of the American Civil War, Cuban slavers lost the acquiescence of the U.S. government; and Spanish officials, as part of an effort to stave off American interest in conquering Cuba, enforced the trade's abolition.

WHAT EXPLAINS BRITISH ANTISLAVERY?

Through the first decades of the 19th century, antislavery remained the concern of broad segments of the British public. Galvanized in part by major slave revolts in Barbados (1816), Guyana (1823), and Jamaica (1831–32)—which suggested that the system was impossible to sustain—the abolitionist movement made increasingly powerful use of its old tools of published tracts, rallies, petitions, and political lobbying, now attacking slavery itself. In 1833, Parliament received more than 5,000 petitions with almost 1.5 million signatures, including a sewn and pasted petition half a mile long, signed by some 350,000 women. After the 1832 Reform Act significantly broadened voting for Parliamentary elections, new MPs who favored abolition were elected. In 1833, Parliament passed a bill that emancipated nearly 800,000 colonial slaves as of August 1, 1834, compensating their owners with the immense sum of 20 million pounds sterling. After four years of "apprenticeship," in which ex-slaves were forced to do unpaid labor for former masters, final freedom came to slaves in the British Empire in 1838.

Then and later, Britons and many Americans hailed the Emancipation Act as one of the greatest humanitarian achievements in history. In 1869 the historian W. E. H. Lecky famously wrote that "The unwearied, unostentatious, and inglorious crusade of England against slavery may probably be regarded as among the three or four perfectly virtuous acts recorded in the history of nations." For at least a century, historians attributed the end of Britain's slave trade and slavery to the divine inspiration and formidable efforts of Wilberforce, Clarkson, Sharp, and the other so-called "Saints," even if they did note that the appalling, slave-like conditions of English workers never received quite the same attention as West Indian slaves did.

In 1944, however, a West Indian scholar named Eric Williams (who later became prime minister of Trinidad) published *Capitalism and Slavery*, a forceful challenge to the notion that British antislavery was an entirely humanitarian movement. Williams made two broad arguments that still generate debate among historians. First, he maintained that profits from the slave trade and/or the entire slave system provided much of the capital that financed the English Industrial Revolution (a thesis that will be examined in the epilogue, "Making Connections"). Additionally, Williams argued that British capitalism, initially created in part by slavery, ultimately led to slavery's demise. West Indian economies, he essentially argued, were in decline by the late 18th century, sustained only by a protected British market for their goods. As Britain's economy became increasingly industrialized and reliant on free trade around the world, capitalists and their allies in Parliament turned against the mercantilism which sustained slavery. Although Williams gave credit to the "brilliant band" of abolitionists who worked to end slavery, their efforts were successful, he argued, because they were in accord with the new economic necessities of free-trade capitalism.

As early as 1776, Adam Smith's *Wealth of Nations*, with its emphasis on the benefits of free trade and wage labor, had raised doubts about the economic wisdom of Britain's highly protected imperial slave system. But more recently, several economic historians have refuted Williams' second thesis by showing that the economy of the British West Indies was vibrant, and indeed expanding, up to the time of abolition. Rather than reflecting British economic interests, in fact, antislavery policies were enormously harmful to them. Still, Williams' skepticism about the motives behind British abolitionism suggested an important question: why, if slavery could be abolished simply because people began to think it was immoral, did this happen only in the late 18th/early 19th centuries, and principally in Britain? Could Britons of that time period really have such a monopoly on moral virtue? Or could it be that other particularities of the time and place help to account for such a dramatic, historically unprecedented shift in majority opinion?

Even if the Industrial Revolution, centered in Britain at the same time as the antislavery movement gained momentum, did not create *economic* imperatives for the abolition of slavery and the slave trade, some historians have argued convincingly that it created the *ideological* conditions that made antislavery popular and possible. In the United Kingdom and, not incidentally, the Northern United States, people began to equate free wage labor with progress and to link individual freedom with general prosperity. Their own societies were experiencing rapid economic growth without domestic slavery, people could reason, so clearly slavery was not *necessary* for social advancement, and it might even retard progress. Furthermore, by the late 18th century both skilled workers and their employers needed to dignify and defend wage labor, which had been denigrated for ages but was expanding dramatically with industrialization. A common crusade against slavery not only helped to ennoble "free" labor, but it also provided ideological kinship between the type of people who paid wages and those who received them. Emphasizing the ideological context of antislavery does not diminish the credit due to abolitionists for their accomplishments, but it also explains why their efforts bore fruit when and where they did.

CONCLUSION

Confronted in 1820 with Osei Bonsu's skeptical query about why the British no longer traded in slaves, Joseph Dupuis "was confessedly at a loss for an argument that might pass as a satisfactory reason." "The king did not deem it plausible," he recounted, "that this obnoxious traffic should have been abolished from motives of humanity alone."

Over a century later, historians began to raise questions similar to Osei Bonsu's. They pointed out the coincidental timing between antislavery and the rise of industrial capitalism in Britain, as well as the apparent contradiction between moral indignation about slavery and harsh treatment of the British poor. Historians also credit enslaved West Indians with pushing Britain toward abolition. Massive slave revolts not only in Haiti but also in British colonies convinced policy-makers that if they did not abolish slavery voluntarily, the slaves would seize freedom for themselves.

Yet a new humanitarianism in the late 18th and early 19th centuries did help sow the seeds of abolition. Influenced by Enlightenment rationality and Evangelical Christianity, some people were beginning to question whether kings deserved to rule and whether God really favored some over others; in the process, they began to think that slavery was wrong. Amid this ideological change, Granville Sharp, Thomas Clarkson, William Wilberforce, Olaudah Equiano, and others dedicated their lives to the struggle for abolition. After thousands of years in which slavery as an institution was not even questioned, they convinced the world's most powerful slave trader to abolish it. They did so by creating the first massive grassroots movement for political change, mobilizing millions of British citizens to sign petitions, contribute money, attend meetings and rallies, boycott sugar, and campaign for reformist political candidates. Few of the movement's supporters had ever even laid eyes on the West Indies or an enslaved person. Most of them held assumptions about race, class, and gender that many of us would find bothersome today. Still, their concern for fellow human beings separated from them by distance, language, culture, and appearance—a sense of empathy nurtured by the antislavery activists—should remain as an example for us all.

SOURCES

■ **Slavery and the Rights of Man**

In this essay, published in 1775 in *The Pennsylvania Journal and the Weekly Advertiser,* the anti-colonial pamphleteer Thomas Paine challenged colonists' justifications for the enslavement of Africans. As you read it, consider how Paine marshaled the same kinds of arguments Americans used against the British government to oppose the slave trade. What is wrong with the slave trade in Paine's view? Moreover, what views does Paine seem to hold about Africans? Can you infer from Paine's approach some of the arguments others were making in favor of the slave trade? How does he link the goals of the American Revolution to antislavery?

TO AMERICANS

That some desperate wretches should be wiling to steal and enslave men by violence and murder for gain, is rather lamentable than strange. But that many civilized, nay, Christianized people should approve, and be concerned in the savage practice, is surprising; and still persist, though it has been so often proved contrary to the light of nature, to every principle of Justice and Humanity, and even good policy, by a succession of eminent men, and several late publications.

Our Traders in MEN (an unnatural commodity!) must know the wickedness of that SLAVE-TRADE, if they attend to reasoning, or the dictates of their own hearts; and such as shun and stifle all these, willfully sacrifice Conscience, and the character of integrity to that golden idol.

The Managers of that Trade themselves, and others, testify, that many of these African nations inhabit fertile countries, are industrious farmers, enjoy plenty, and lived quietly, adverse to war, before the Europeans debauched them with liquors, and bribing them against one another; and that these inoffensive people are brought into slavery, by stealing them, tempting Kings to sell subjects, which they have no right to do, and hiring one tribe to war against another. . . . By such wicked and inhuman ways the English are said to enslave towards one hundred thousand yearly. . . .

Most shocking of all is alleging the Sacred Scriptures to favour this wicked practice. One would have thought none but infidel cavilers[2] would endeavor to make them appear contrary to the plain

---

Source: Thomas Paine, "African Slavery in America," *The Pennsylvania Journal and the Weekly Advertiser,* March 8, 1775.

[2]Non-Christians or false Christians who argue invalid positions.

dictates of natural light, and Conscience, in a matter of common Justice and Humanity, which they cannot be. . . . As much in vain, perhaps, will they search ancient history for examples of the modern Slave-Trade. Too many nations enslaved the prisoners they took in war. But to go to nations with whom there is no war . . . purely to catch inoffensive people, like wild beasts, for slaves, is an height of outrage against Humanity and Justice, that seems left by Heathen nations to be practiced by pretended Christians. How shameful are all attempts to colour and excuse it! As these people are not convicted of forfeiting freedom, they still have a natural, perfect right to it; and the Governments whenever they come should, in justice set them free, and punish those who hold them in slavery. . . .

But the chief design of this paper is . . . to entreat Americans to consider. . . . With what consistency, or decency, they complain so loudly of attempts to enslave them, while they hold so many hundred thousands in slavery; and annually enslave many thousands more, without the pretence of authority, or claim upon them?

■ Revolution in St. Domingue

Thomas Clarkson, England's foremost abolitionist activist, published this pamphlet in London in 1792 as the French and Haitian Revolutions stalled the movement against the slave trade. Part of his goal was to refute the idea, then circulating among pro-slavery advocates, that abolitionists had directly or indirectly caused the slave rebellion in St. Domingue. As you read the excerpt below, note Clarkson's use, like Paine's, of the concept of natural rights. What did cause the St. Domingue slave revolt, in Clarkson's estimation? Furthermore, why does he think that abolition of the slave trade will be good for planters in Britain's island colonies? What will happen if abolition is postponed?

. . . To what cause then may we attribute the insurrections in the Islands? Undoubtedly to the Slave Trade, in consequence of which thousands are annually poured into the Islands, who have been fraudulently and forcibly deprived of the Rights of Men. All these come into them, of course, with dissatisfied and exasperated minds; and this discontent and feeling of resentment must be farther heightened by the treatment which people coming into them under such a situation must unavoidably receive; for we cannot keep people in a state

---

Source: Thomas Clarkson, *The True State of the Case, Respecting the Insurrection at St. Domingo* (Published in London, 1792).

of subjection to us, who acknowledge no obligation whatever to serve us, but by breaking their spirits and treating them as creatures of another species. . . .

As, however, the present insurrection in St. Domingo is somewhat connected with the late Revolution in France, it may be necessary to say a few words upon it as relative to that event. . . . Here then we see no less than three factions prevalent at the same moment in St. Domingo. The Whites divided into two parties; and the White and People of Colour burning with a fury hardly satiable by the extirpation of one another. What then did the negroes do at this interesting moment? Seeing their Lords and Masters not able to agree among themselves, but at daggers drawn with one another, they determined to take advantage of the divisions among them, and to assert their violated rights by force of arms.—Such is the true state of the case respecting the Insurrection at St. Domingo, and what do we learn from it but the following truth? "That the slave trade, and the oppression naturally resulting from it, was the real and only cause of this Insurrection," as it ever has been, and ever will be, of similar events; but that the Revolution in France, by causing the three divisions before mentioned, did afford the Negroes an opportunity which they would otherwise not so easily have found, of endeavoring to vindicate for themselves the unalterable Rights of Man.

The above accounts then lead us to three separate conclusions: First, That the Slave Trade is the real cause of all West Indian Insurrections.—Secondly, that as long as it exists, so long may these Insurrections be expected.—And Thirdly, That the St. Domingo Insurrection, in particular, so far from affording us a just argument (as the Planters say) to discontinue our exertions at the present moment, calls upon us to redouble them, if we have any value for our own islands, or any wish that the present Proprietors of them may preserve their estates to themselves, and perpetuate them to their posterity.

■ An African Describes the Horrors of Slavery

Olaudah Equiano's now-famous narrative, first published in 1793, was the most important written work to emerge from the movement to abolish the British slave trade. Although scholars now dispute Equiano's African origins, there is no doubt that his poignant story of

---

Source: The Interesting Narrative of Olaudah Equiano, or Gustavus Vassa the African, Written by Himself (London, 1789), excerpts from Chapter 5.

enslavement, slavery, and struggles after manumission derived much of its power from its acceptance as a firsthand account.

The following excerpt deals with the period in the early 1760s when Equiano, a young man, served as the slave of a sea captain based at Montserrat, in the West Indies. Equiano traveled by boat all around the Caribbean, observing the condition and treatment of slaves in a variety of settings. As you read, keep in mind Equiano's purpose in writing. How do his narrative choices serve his political goals? What ideals does he implicitly hold to be universal? What information and images does he convey about slavery? What impression does he create of slaves, slave-owners and overseers, slave traders, and the slave trade itself?

. . . While I was thus employed by my master [on merchant ships] I was often a witness to cruelties of every kind, which were exercised on my unhappy fellow slaves. I used frequently to have different cargoes of new negroes in my care for sale; and it was almost a constant practice with our clerks, and other whites, to commit violent depredations on the chastity of the female slaves; and these I was, though with reluctance, obliged to submit to at all times, being unable to help them. . . . And yet in Montserrat I have seen a negro man staked to the ground, and cut most shockingly, and then his ears cut off bit by bit, because he had been connected with a white woman who was a common prostitute: as if it were no crime in the whites to rob an innocent African girl of her virtue; but most heinous in a black man only to gratify a passion of nature, where the temptation was offered by one of a different colour, though the most abandoned woman of her species. Another negro man was half hanged, and then burnt, for attempting to poison a cruel overseer. Thus by repeated cruelties are the wretched first urged to despair, and then murdered, because they still retain so much of human nature about them as to wish to put an end to their misery, and retaliate on their tyrants!

. . . Nor was such usage as this confined to particular places or individuals; for, in all the different islands in which I have been (and I have visited no less than fifteen) the treatment of the slaves was nearly the same; so nearly indeed, that the history of an island, or even a plantation, with a few such exceptions as I have mentioned, might serve for a history of the whole. Such a tendency has the slave-trade to debauch men's minds, and harden them to every feeling of humanity! For I will not suppose that the dealers in slaves are born worse than other men—No; it is the fatality of this mistaken avarice, that it corrupts the milk of human kindness and turns it into gall. And, had the pursuits of those men been different, they might have been as generous, as tender-hearted and just, as they are unfeeling, rapacious and cruel. Surely this traffic cannot be good, which spreads like a pestilence, and taints what it touches!

■ The British Antislavery Squadron

As the British government attempted to suppress the Atlantic slave trade after its own 1808 ban, naval squadrons patrolled the African coast, intercepting slave ships en route to the Americas. Samuel Ajayi Crowther, who later became an Anglican bishop and scholar well known throughout West Africa, was rescued from slavery by a British Navy ship and resettled at Sierra Leone. Crowther had been a young teenager when his household was caught up in the Yoruba wars of the early 19th century. Captured in March 1821, he spent the next nine months bound to several different masters and being moved toward the coast. At Lagos, he was sold to Portuguese traders, who loaded him onto a ship bound for Brazil several months later, in April 1822.

The excerpt below is from an account of his capture and ordeal that Crowther originally prepared in 1837, at the request of missionaries in Sierra Leone. What does it tell you about Crowther's fears and discomforts? What was his initial perception of the English sailors? Why do you think he described his revenge on his Portuguese former owner as wicked? And finally, how did he get to Sierra Leone?

About this time, intelligence was given that the English were cruising the coast. This was another subject of sorrow with us—that there must be war also on the sea as well as on land—a thing never heard of before, or imagined practicable. This delayed our embarkation. . . .

After a few weeks' delay, we embarked, at night in canoes, from Lagos to the beach; and on the following morning were put on board

---

Source: J. F. Ade Ajayi, "Samuel Ajayi Crowther of Oyo," in Philip D. Curtin (ed.), *Africa Remembered: Narratives by West Africans from the Era of the Slave Trade* (Prospect Heights, IL: Waveland Press, 1997 [1967]), pp. 311–14.

the vessel, which immediately sailed away. The crew being busy embarking us, 187 in number, had no time to give us either breakfast or supper; and we, being unaccustomed to the motion of the vessel, employed the whole of this day in sea-sickness. . . . On the very same evening, we were surprised by two English men-of-war; and on the next morning found ourselves in the hands of new conquerors, whom we at first very much dreaded, they being armed with long swords. In the morning, being called up from the hold, we were astonished to find ourselves among two very large men-of-war and several other brigs. . . .

Our owner was bound with his sailors; except the cook, who was preparing our breakfast. . . . Now we began to entertain a good opinion of our conquerors. Very soon after breakfast we were divided into several of the vessels around us. This was now cause of new fears, not knowing where our misery would end. . . .

In a few days we [Crowther and his companions] were quite at home in the man-of-war. . . . Our Portuguese owner and his son were brought over into the same vessel, bound in fetters; and, thinking that I should no more get into his hand, I had the boldness to strike him on the head, while he was shaving by his son—an act, however, very wicked and unkind in its nature. His vessel was towed along by the man-of-war, with the remainder of the slaves therein. . . .

. . . After nearly two months and a half cruising on the coast, we were landed at Sierra Leone, on the 17th of June 1822. . . . Here we had the pleasure of meeting many of our country people, but none were known before. They assured us of our liberty and freedom; and we very soon believed them. . . .

Epilogue: Making Connections
Legacies of the Atlantic Slave Trade

THE SLAVE TRADE IN MODERN MEMORY

Two centuries after the transatlantic slave trade was first abolished, modern Americans, Europeans, and Africans grapple with its legacies. During a 1991 visit to Senegal's Gorée Island slave fort, for instance, Pope John Paul II apologized "for the sins of Christian Europe against Africa." In the early 1990s, the Organization of African Unity (OAU) embraced the idea of claiming atonement for slavery and colonialism. In 1993, a pan-African conference on reparations held in Nigeria determined that the damage caused by slavery, colonialism, and neo-colonialism "is not a thing of the past, but is painfully manifest in the damaged lives of contemporary Africans from Harlem to Harare, in the damaged economies of the black world from Guinea to Guyana, from Somalia to Suriname." The conference called for monetary reparations, that the slave trade be designated a crime against humanity, and that the former slave-trading nations apologize for it. A United Nations conference on racism, held in South Africa in 2001, labeled the slave trade a crime against humanity, but fell short of urging reparations or specific apologies from European nations. And the UN General Assembly proclaimed 2004 as the "International Year to Commemorate the Struggle against Slavery and Its Abolition."

Leaders of European cities and countries previously associated with the slave trade have also begun to address its memory. In 1999, the Liverpool City Council passed a formal motion apologizing for the city's part in the slave trade. In 2001, the French Senate recognized slavery as a crime against humanity; five years later French people in numerous cities held ceremonies for Slavery Remembrance Day. Also in 2006, the Church of England voted to apologize to the descendants of the victims of the slave trade, and Britain's Prime Minister voiced his "deep sorrow" over Britain's role in slaving. In perhaps the most theatrical display of atonement, in June of 2006, a descendant of England's first slave trader, Sir John Hawkins (whose account is included in Chapter 2), knelt in chains in front of a crowd of 25,000 Africans and asked forgiveness for his ancestor's actions. The Vice President of the Gambia, where this ceremony took place, accepted the apology and then came forward to remove the chains. There have been fewer re-examinations of the role Africans played in the export of other Africans. But the government of Ghana, whose slave-trading castles have become major tourist destinations, has issued an apology for participation in the slave trade, along with an invitation to members of the African diaspora to reconnect with the land of their ancestors.

In the United States, the memory and legacy of slavery have at times been connected to calls for reparations to descendants of slaves. Shortly after the Civil War ended in 1865, General William Sherman ordered that land on the Georgia and South Carolina coasts be set aside for the settlement of thousands of newly freed families—the famous "forty acres and a mule" idea. But the promise was quickly recanted, and the land was taken back, with no other plans for reparations made. Civil rights activists have revisited the issue since then. In 1963, for example, Martin Luther King, Jr., called Sherman's promise "a check which has come back marked 'insufficient funds.'" Some critics suggest, however, that reparations would be neither feasible nor fair. Not only are former slaveholders and former slaves all dead; their descendants do not fall into neatly identifiable, separate groups. Moreover, most of today's Americans have no ancestral connection to antebellum slavery at all. Instead of urging monetary reparations, leaders of some American cities and states have passed laws requiring businesses to reveal their historic involvement in slavery, which some banks, insurers, and other companies have done. Universities—most notably Brown University in Providence, Rhode Island and the University of North Carolina at Chapel Hill—have also begun to examine their historical connections to the slave trade and slavery.

Contemporary debates about apologies and reparations are based on the obvious presumption that the slave trade and slavery benefited some at the expense of others, and that these imbalances have had lasting effects. But understanding the nature and extent of those discrepancies requires the study of history. How did the forced migration of more than 10 million Africans to the Americas over some 400 years shape the world we currently live in? Among the different groups of actors presented in this book, which do you think gained the most from the Atlantic slave trade? Which suffered the most harm?

What if you look beyond groups of individuals to the level of societies or countries—then what patterns of winners and losers emerge? How did the connections between enslaved Africans, the rulers and merchants who sold them, the captains and crews who transported them, the Euro-Americans who purchased them, and the mainly Europeans who financed and organized the entire operation affect both individual lives and fortunes, as well as large-scale economic, social, and political transformations? As the 21st century begins, Western Europeans and North Americans enjoy some of the highest standards of living on the globe. In contrast, approximately half of all Africans live on $1 a day or less. Most of the world's poorest countries are African. To what extent does the history of the slave trade and slavery explain the huge economic gap between Africa and the West?

AFRICA

Some of the slave trade's effects on African economies were discussed in Chapter 2. Although individual kings and merchants gained power and wealth through the export of captives, Africans on the whole suffered. European imports like textiles and metals may have inhibited local manufacturing, although probably not on a large scale.

More significantly, given the importance of "wealth in people" for economic development, the outright loss of some 20 million people and their descendants deprived West and Central African societies of farm produce, animal husbandry, crafts, specialized skills, administrative talent, and entrepreneurial creativity on a scale that can only be imagined. Moreover, the violence and insecurity endured by people at the slaving frontiers inhibited farming and other productive activities.

The perpetuation, and indeed expansion, of slavery within Africa during and after the period of the Atlantic slave trade ultimately became one of the justifications for European imperialism. As the slave trade came to an end, Africans began to be perceived not so much as the slave trade's victims but as its perpetrators. This was how Europeans explained to themselves the continued supply of slaves from Africa and the continued use of slavery within Africa. European, particularly British, officials became convinced that outside intervention was necessary to promote legitimate commerce and put African slave dealers out of business. In the Bight of Benin, for instance, British gunboats bombarded the busy slave port of Lagos in 1851. Ten years later, again citing antislavery justifications, British agents deposed the Lagos king, installed his rival as nominal ruler, and declared Lagos to be a British colony. Lagos remained under British rule—as the administrative and commercial center of colonial Nigeria—for the next century. In East Africa in the 1850s and 1860s, the explorer and missionary David Livingstone observed slave caravans traveling through the hinterland to the coast. In 1873, he famously called for "anyone who will help to heal this open sore of the world."

By the time of the Berlin Conference of 1884–85, which historians see as the start of the "scramble for Africa," the British and other Europeans tended to see Africa as a center of evil, a part of the world represented by slavery and cannibalism, which it was their duty to "civilize." Along with drawing the boundaries of their future African empires, participants at the conference condemned the slave trade and pledged to undertake antislavery measures in their new colonies. In 1890, Belgium's King Leopold II sponsored a conference in Brussels with the intention "of putting an end to the crimes and devastations engendered by the traffic in African slaves, of efficiently protecting the aboriginal population of Africa, and of securing for that vast continent all the benefits of peace and civilization." Within a couple of years King Leopold was the sole and personal proprietor of the entire Congo Free State. By the end of the 19th century, Britain, France, Germany, Belgium, Portugal, and even Italy colonized nearly every corner of the African continent, continuing a process of wealth transfer that had begun during the slave trade (Map E.1).

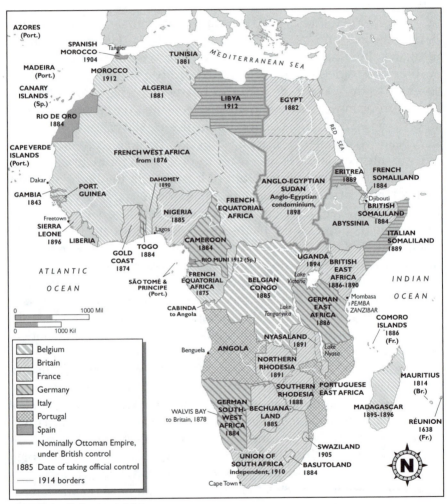

MAP E.1 Colonized Africa

Source: http://www.homestead.com/wysinger/WALL5295874_op_800x548.jpg.

GREAT BRITAIN

During the same centuries in which African societies were undermined by the slave trade, Great Britain began to experience a revolutionary series of related economic and social transformations. Increased population, pressures on rural dwellers to seek wage employment, mercantile policies, stunning technological innovations, the elaboration of new business systems: all of these and more brought industrialization— unevenly and haltingly, to be sure—to the United Kingdom beginning in the 18th century. In Britain before anywhere else, urban or manufacturing employment overtook rural, agrarian life. While 18 percent of the male labor force worked in industry in 1688, by 1847 the proportion had increased to 47 percent. At the same time, though agriculture grew in absolute terms, it accounted for a declining share of national income: 45 percent in 1770, compared to 20 percent in 1851. Such developments inaugurated a new pattern of society, creating classes of workers and industrialists who lived permanently in the growing cities, along with innumerable related changes.

Was it simply a coincidence that Great Britain was the first industrial nation, the 18th-century world's greatest slave trader, and the hub of a large, slave-driven empire? How important were the profits of the slave trade and colonial slavery to British economic growth? In his landmark book *Capitalism and Slavery* (1944), historian and Trinidadian statesman Eric Williams argued that the slave trade and its adjuncts, in fact, provided much of the initial capital that brought about England's Industrial Revolution. Plantation owners, shipbuilders, and merchants connected with the slave trade, he suggested, accumulated vast fortunes that established banks and heavy industry in Europe, and expanded the reach of capitalism worldwide. The "triangular trade," as Williams put it, "fertilized the entire productive system of the country."

Since that book was published it has faced challenges by historians skeptical that the Atlantic trade and/or the plantation economies made decisive contributions to British industrialization. One piece of their debate has focused on the extent to which profits from the slave trade or slavery financed initial investments in capitalist projects. In the late 18th and early 19th centuries, British public and private investors undertook a major series of development projects: in the merchant marine, in harbors and docks, in canals, in agricultural improvements, and in new industrial machinery. According to some economic historians, nearly all of the initial capital for these programs came from the profits of local agriculture or European commerce, not slavery and slave trading. Yet the profits of empire and slavery were crucial, other historians suggest, in supplementing the resources of public authorities, landlords, merchants, and manufacturers, especially since available capital was limited by a rising population and heavy military spending.

Scholars are in broader agreement that, regardless of the importance of empire and slavery in providing the initial capital for industrialization, Britain's slave-worked colonies and slave suppliers were crucial trading partners for the newly emerging industrialists. Both Africa and the Americas provided a protected and growing market for English-made or English-traded products. English exports to Africa and the Americas, in fact, increased tenfold during the 18th century. By the 1790s—that is, even after the American Revolution—New World markets accounted for two-thirds of all British exports. Especially since British workers often did not earn enough to buy the goods their factories produced, overseas trade in general and colonial demand in particular kept the industrial economy humming. Moreover, 18th- and 19th-century industrialization was heavily concentrated in the textile sector. Slave plantations were the principal suppliers of raw cotton, without which the factories would have been idle. Cotton imports to Great Britain quadrupled between 1785 and 1805 alone, despite rising prices.

Colonial slavery also contributed to the growth of British capitalism by stimulating new wants among consumers. Their increasing taste for commodities like sugar, coffee, tobacco, and cotton, above and beyond their subsistence needs, gave ordinary Britons incentives to work for wages. Ironically, it was slave-grown sugar that initially increased Britain's consumer-oriented market. England's annual sugar consumption increased from around 10,000 tons in 1700 to 80,000 tons in 1800 when, with the population of Great Britain at less than 11 million, average consumption of sugar per person must have been around 16 lb per year, compared to 4 lb per year in 1700. Cookbooks of the time show that sugar was no longer regarded as a luxury, but instead a common ingredient and an everyday taste. People spooned sugar into popular new, imported beverages like tea, coffee, and chocolate, some of them also grown by colonial slaves.

But if the slave trade and colonial slavery promoted industrialization in Britain, one may ask, why did it not do so elsewhere, like in

France or Portugal? In fact, those counterexamples show that slave trading or control of a slave-based empire was not enough by itself to bring industrial transformation. Britain's large commercial empire, integrated economy, and coal deposits, along with a government that promoted mercantile and manufacturing interests without imposing too much control, already gave it economic advantages over its European rivals. Combined with these factors, New World slavery and the trade associated with it helped create British industrialism.

By 1800 there were nearly 800,000 slaves in Britain's plantation colonies, compared to 857,000 slaves in the United States, about 1.5 million in Brazil, and around 250,000 in Spanish America. Working under compulsion, the enslaved men, women, and children on British plantations toiled for an average of 2,500 to 3,000 hours per year and each produced crops worth around £18, or £14,400,000 in total. The greater part of the money paid for the plantation crops they produced returned to Britain as mercantile profit, planters' profit, customs' duties, expenditures for new materials on the plantations, and so on. Thus sugar, tobacco, and cotton which had cost the slaves some 2,200,000,000 hours of toil was sold by metropolitan merchants or manufacturers to consumers who, in order to afford these purchases, themselves had to labor for untold millions of hours for their employers. Although slave-owners were compensated some £20 million at the time of British emancipation, the enslaved were not paid for their contributions to British economic development. In fact, as discussed below, their fortunes scarcely improved with emancipation.

THE AMERICAS

Throughout the Americas, whether slaveholders were compensated for their losses with emancipation or not, the enslaved themselves received virtually nothing. Yet their unpaid labor was largely what made European settlement and development in the New World possible. The production of Caribbean and South American sugar, Brazilian and Cuban coffee, Brazilian gold, and North American cotton—commodities at the center of the Atlantic economy—were all dependent upon Africans and their descendants. Thus, the past and present development of the Americas was based on an institution whose labor came free of charge and entailed enormous suffering. Does this historical debt require some contemporary restitution?

The West Indies

We've already seen how important the profits of West Indian plantations were to the development of Britain's economy. Yet, after the abolition of slavery in the West Indies, estate owners struggled with labor shortages. Former slaves were unwilling to work on plantations under the terms planters offered, and they concentrated instead on subsistence agriculture. Sugar production plummeted. Planters and policy-makers desperately looked for alternative sources of plantation labor, turning primarily to Asia. Beginning even before the abolition of slavery, the British government organized a regular system of contract labor in cooperation with the British colonial government of India. Indian labor recruits signed contracts to migrate and work in the plantation colonies for a period of three, five, or sometimes ten years. Although contract labor might seem more humane than slavery, often it was similar in practice. The contractor could sell the laborer's contract to a third party without his consent; default on the contract could land a laborer in jail; and although physical punishment with a whip was not legal, it was common. But contract workers were paid a small wage—below the market rate—and they did have some recourse to the court system, which slaves never had. At the end of the contract, the worker was usually entitled to return transportation, although relatively few received it. Most Indian laborers ended up staying in the island colonies to work for (low) wages. Between 1845 and 1914, India supplied nearly 450,000 contract workers for the British West Indies, as well others for the French Caribbean. For the Caribbean as a whole, the number of non-African coerced laborers imported in the 19th century slightly exceeded the number of Africans who came in by way of the illegal slave trade.

Meanwhile, in the decades after emancipation, planters also took steps to reassert their control over the African-descended laboring population. White elites, especially in Jamaica, used their political power to impose a series of restrictions on freed people's movement, "squatting" (i.e., settlement on land that they did not officially own), and use of plantation property. After a short-lived rise in wages, planters managed to lower them again as well as reestablish their ownership of provision grounds (where slaves had grown their own food). They maintained labor discipline through vagrancy laws, penal sanctions for abrogated contracts, and a reintroduction of corporal punishment. They maintained political power, in spite of Afro-Jamaicans' stark numerical advantage, by manipulating the system of government and imposing a tax on voting (a poll tax) in 1859.

Although African-descended workers staged violent revolts against planter oppression in Dominica, Guyana, St. Vincent, Tobago, and Barbados, the largest uprising took place at Morant Bay, in Jamaica, in 1865. Under the leadership of a lay preacher named Paul Bogle, some 1,500–2,000 rebels burned plantations and attacked planters and government officials, attempting to take control over the region themselves. Defeated by the government's maroon allies, who were still obligated by treaty to help suppress revolts, the peasants then faced terrible vengeance. Bogle was one of nearly 500 killed, while hundreds were flogged and 1,000 houses were burned by government forces operating under martial law. The repression was so vicious that the British government dispatched a royal commission to Jamaica to investigate the actions of its chief architect, Governor Eyre. The commissioners ultimately condemned Eyre's "wanton and cruel" repression of the rebellion; yet in 1866, the British government abolished the Jamaica Assembly on the grounds that elected self-government was not appropriate for a colony composed mainly of descendants of slaves.

The Morant Bay uprising marked a turning point in official thinking about race. Earlier, British reformers had stressed the possible improvement of those of African descent, even if they seemed less cultivated than Europeans. Africans were often depicted as "noble savages" and their descendants, degraded by slavery, were nonetheless part of a shared humanity. "Am I not a man and a brother?" was practically the motto of the abolitionist movement. But as the Jamaican economy faltered after the end of slavery, British observers' views began to change, and they began to see emancipation as a failure. Blacks refused to work on sugar estates at the wages planters felt they could afford to pay. This was then seen simply as "blacks will not work on sugar estates." From that they reasoned, "blacks will not work." As struggles over labor and political rights became increasingly frequent, climaxing in the Morant Bay Rebellion, planters and British officials became convinced that black people—not just Afro-Jamaicans, but Africans and their descendants everywhere—were lazy and dangerous, incapable of responsible citizenship.

The United States

In contrast to the British West Indies, the profits of North American slavery stayed in the United States, helping to grow what would become the Western world's largest economy. And in contrast to Brazil and Cuba, where the closing of the slave trade made it impossible to replenish or increase the numbers of enslaved individuals, slavery in the United States expanded dramatically even after fresh supplies from Africa were cut off. Higher reproduction rates and declining rates of manumission meant that the slave population of the United States was the only one that was growing in the mid-19th century, as Figure E.1 shows. Between 1800 and 1860 the number of enslaved African Americans quadrupled, from 1 million to 4 million, largely because of natural increase. Their total value in 1860 was $3.5 billion—the equivalent of $68.4 billion today. As investment capital, the value of North American slaves far exceeded the cash value of all the farms in the Southern states and represented three times the cost of constructing all the railroads that then existed in the United States.

Although slaves toiled in many sectors of the American economy, in the 19th century they were massively concentrated in cotton production. The cotton gin, invented in the 1790s, could clean 50 pounds of raw cotton per day, compared to 1 pound per day by hand; and the territorial expansion of the United States (six new slave states were added between 1792 and 1821) made abundant land with

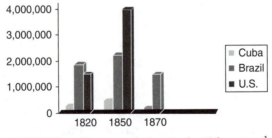

FIGURE E.1   Slave populations in the 19th century[1]

---

[1]Compiled from information in Leslie Bethell (ed.), *Brazil: Empire and Republic, 1822–1930* (Cambridge: Cambridge University Press, 1989); Rebecca J. Scott, *Slave Emancipation in Cuba: The Transition to Free Labor, 1860–1899* (Princeton: Princeton University Press, 1985); and David Brion Davis, *Inhuman Bondage: The Rise and Fall of Slavery in the New World* (Oxford: Oxford University Press, 2006).

an appropriate climate available in the Lower South. Enticed by the prospects of cotton production in this new American frontier, slaveholders from Virginia and Maryland sent or brought about a million slaves south and west—largely to Georgia, Alabama, and Mississippi—between 1789 and 1860. Two-thirds of these enslaved people were sold in the internal American slave trade, often separating from families and communities in the process. Southern investment flowed mainly into the purchase of slaves, who became the major form of Southern wealth aside from land.

Southern slaves and slaveholders participated in a global economic system based on international demand for cotton, centered on the British textile industry. By 1840, the South grew more than 60 percent of the world's cotton, supplying mills and markets from Manchester to Moscow and enriching not only Southern planters but also Northern bankers, insurers, commission agents, and shipowners. Through the antebellum period, cotton accounted for more than half the value of all American exports, thus financing the major share of the nation's imports and investment capital. The large planters ranked among America's richest and most politically influential men. By 1860, two-thirds of the wealthiest Americans lived in the South. In a very real way, the economy and society of the entire country was shaped by Southern slavery.

Although the Civil War ultimately ended slavery in the United States, Union leaders were not committed to emancipation from the start. Abraham Lincoln personally opposed slavery, but he initially favored gradual emancipation and the colonization of African Americans abroad. After South Carolina's legislators led other Southerners in seceding from the Union in 1861, he and other Northern lawmakers worried that any radical policy against slavery would alienate Unionists in the South and also Union supporters in the border states like Maryland and Delaware. "I have no purpose to interfere with the institution of slavery in the States where it exists," Lincoln stated shortly after the war began.

As in the American Revolution, however, enslaved people realized that the war offered opportunities for freedom. From the beginning of hostilities, refugees from slavery made their way to Union Army camps. At first, commanders not only refused to aid escaped slaves but even returned them to their Confederate owners. When it became clear that the Confederacy was using slave labor to build fortifications, however, Northern generals began to treat fugitives as "contraband of war" and used them as laborers and other support personnel. In many cases escapees were able to provide valuable military intelligence. In 1862, Congress formally prohibited the use of Union troops to return fugitive slaves.

A war against slavery may not have been what Union leaders originally intended, but political and military considerations increasingly favored abolition. Perhaps most importantly, the war took an enormous human toll. In the North alone, with a population of 20 million in 1860, about 2.1 million men served in the armed forces, or more than one in ten people. Eventually the Union side lost 360,000 men, a number roughly equivalent to 5.4 million deaths today. President Lincoln began to see the abolition of slavery as a military necessity for saving the Union. Moreover, antislavery sentiment was gaining political influence in the North and among Republicans. In 1862, Congress approved a bill abolishing slavery in Washington, D.C., with compensation to the owners. More than 3,000 slaves were freed, at a cost to the government of $300 each. On January 1, 1863, Lincoln issued his famous Emancipation Proclamation, declaring that slaves held in rebel-controlled areas were free. Abolitionist Frederick Douglass publicly congratulated Lincoln "upon what may be called the greatest event of our nation's history." From then on, as the Union Army advanced, so did emancipation. Federal troops welcomed fugitive slaves, who continued to flock to the "contraband" camps set up within Union lines.

The Emancipation Proclamation also called for enlisting African American troops, a process already begun in the border states. There, the recruitment of African American soldiers, with a promise of freedom for them and their families, destroyed slavery even before legal emancipation had been enacted. Altogether, by the end of the war over 200,000 African Americans served in the Union armed forces (and 40,000 of them died), forcing most white Americans to recognize the role slaves played in their own liberation. As Lincoln pointed out to critics of his emancipation policy, "You say you will not fight to free negroes. Some of them seem willing to fight for you. . . . If they stake their lives for us, they must be prompted by the strongest motive—the promise of freedom. And the promise being made, must be kept."

Slavery was officially ended in the United States with the ratification of the Thirteenth Amendment to the U.S. Constitution in 1865: "Neither slavery nor involuntary servitude, except as a punishment for crime whereof the party shall have been duly convicted, shall exist within the United States, or any place subject to their jurisdiction." Congress and the states subsequently ratified two more Constitutional amendments, intended to ensure citizenship and voting rights for ex-slaves. During the period of Reconstruction, from 1865 to 1877, freed people and the federal government attempted to remake Southern society on the basis of free labor, equal political rights for blacks and whites, and representative government as outlined in the U.S. Constitution.

But emancipation did not lead to the kind of freedom and equality before the law that abolitionists had envisioned and reconstructionists sought to achieve. White supremacy still permeated the South, and even in the North a commitment to abolition did not mean the absence of racism. After Reconstruction ended, and with it most federal intervention into politics in the ex-Confederacy, Southern leaders enacted *Black Codes* to keep former slaves under control and supervision as if no war had been lost. Outside the formal structures of the law, the Ku Klux Klan and other terrorist groups organized to reinstill white economic, political, and social supremacy. It would be generations before the civil rights movement began to complete the work of emancipation and Reconstruction.

Cuba

The destruction of the largest slave system in the New World isolated the last remaining slave-owners in Cuba and Brazil. In 1862, some 368,000 slaves toiled in Cuba, comprising 27 percent of the total population; Brazilian slaveholders in 1864 held 1,715,000, or 17 percent of the population, in legal bondage. In Cuba and Brazil slavery remained profitable, leading the slave-owners to resort to every device of procrastination against abolitionists at home and abroad, and giving them the resources to do so. Slavery was brought down in these places, as elsewhere, only through slaves' initiatives in the context of a political crisis.

After 1840, with the elimination of Haiti from the international sugar market and steep production declines in the British West Indies, Cuba produced more cane sugar than any other country in the world, while also exporting large quantities of coffee and tobacco. Its plantations came to resemble those in the classic sugar colonies of Jamaica and St. Domingue, with intense exploitation of slave labor, dependence on imports from Africa, and severe repression of resistance. Since the slave population did not reproduce itself, the effective suppression of the African slave trade to Cuba starting in 1866 dealt a dramatic blow to slavery itself. Cuba's slave labor force fell 46 percent between 1862 and 1877, from 368,000 to 199,000. Seeking alternative labor supplies, planters arranged for Chinese contracted workers to be imported; some 150,000 arrived on the island between 1849 and 1875.

In 1868 a liberal revolution in Spain coincided with an armed rebellion in eastern Cuba, far from the major slave plantations in the west, which became known as the Ten Years' War. As in the American Revolution, both the royalist and the rebel sides armed and freed many slaves in exchange for their military support. The best of the rebel generals, Antonio Maceo, in fact was Afro-Cuban. During the war, in 1870, the Spanish government passed a gradual emancipation act called the Moret Law in hopes of winning the support of Afro-Cubans. The law freed all slaves at least 60 years old as well as all children born since September 18, 1868, the date the revolution in Spain began. The real progress toward emancipation during the war, though, was through a multitude of individual emancipations that both sides granted to slaves who joined them. The Cuban slave population dropped by 37 percent during those ten years. After finally suppressing the rebellion, the Spanish government attempted to prolong slavery, organizing an eight-year apprenticeship system in 1880. The system was abandoned in 1886, when all remaining slaves were freed.

After emancipation, planters reorganized sugar production, increasingly using a system of massive central mills supplied under contract by smaller landholders. Cuban wage laborers, tenants, and farmers came in many colors (white, black, brown, and yellow) and often formed cross-ethnic alliances. During Cuba's War for Independence (1895–98), large numbers of former slaves, most of them workers on cane farms and at central sugar mills, enlisted on the side of the rebels, with groups of laborers forming their own units. Independence leaders articulated racial equality as the ideological basis for the movement. The rebel army also featured a number of leaders of color, most famously, again, General Antonio Maceo. In spite of the introduction of American-style racial segregation after the U.S. intervention in 1898, Afro-Cubans' participation in the independence struggle helped to forge nonracial Cuban identity, which was codified in a constitution containing no color restrictions on voting, passed in 1901. Although white supremacy operated in Cuba, sometimes violently, cross-racial alliances continued as well, particularly in the labor movement.

Brazil

More Africans had been transported to Brazil than to any other area of the New World. By the 19th century, however, Brazilian slaves were no longer concentrated in the sugar plantations of the northeast, which were technologically outdated and falling behind Cuban competition. Although a new sugar industry developed along the central coast from the 1870s, Brazil's major export crop and consumer of slaves became coffee. By 1830, Brazil was the world's largest producer of coffee. Along with mining enterprises and some cotton production, the coffee industry was concentrated in the south-central region of the country—São Paulo, Rio de Janeiro, and Minas Gerais. In fact, about 70 percent of Brazil's slave imports in the 19th century went to Rio and São Paulo. Like the cotton-producing Deep South of the United States, central and southern Brazil attracted slaves through a massive internal trade, which persisted even after transatlantic imports ended in the 1850s. In 1822, almost 70 percent of Brazil's slaves lived in the sugar-producing northeast and eastern regions; by 1883, 65 percent were concentrated in the coffee provinces of the south.

High slave death rates and low birth rates, along with individual manumissions and slave self-purchases, meant that in Brazil as in Cuba, the end of the African slave trade brought rapid decline to the slave population. From a high of 3.8 million in 1822, Brazilian slaves numbered 2 to 2.5 million in 1850, 1.5 million in 1873, and 723,000 in 1887, the eve of emancipation. Meanwhile, Brazil's overall population was mushrooming, in large measure because of immigration from Europe, so that slaves occupied a starkly dwindling proportion of the overall population, as Figure E.2 shows. Slaves constituted more than half the Brazilian population in 1822, 15.8 percent of the population in 1872, and only 5 percent in 1888.

As elsewhere, Brazilian planters and their governmental supporters began to establish alternative sources of labor even before slavery was officially abolished. Brazil's available land and employment opportunities, like those of the United States, attracted immigrants from Europe. Some of them—mostly poor immigrants

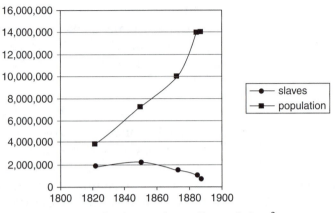

FIGURE E.2   Brazil's slave and overall populations[2]

from Italy, Spain, and Portugal—were offered incentives by the provincial government of São Paulo to accept work on the coffee estates and in other enterprises in the region. By 1872, there were more Portuguese immigrants in Rio de Janeiro than there were slaves. Up to 1888, when slavery ended in Brazil, 590,000 free and subsidized European immigrants arrived in the country, with the majority working on coffee plantations.

As in Cuba, government officials moved against slavery gradually, hoping to deflect abolitionist pressures from abroad while delaying emancipation as long as possible. Brazil's war with Paraguay, fought between 1865 and 1870, brought a new need for arming and freeing blacks as soldiers, which further reduced the size of the naturally declining slave population. In 1871, Brazilian officials passed the Rio Branco Law, a "free womb" measure that made newborn children of slave mothers free and set up a fund to emancipate older children. Since the law actually required the nominally free children of slaves to work under their mothers' masters until they turned 21, it changed very little.

At least until the 1880s, most planters and even middle-class slaveholders saw abolitionism as a treasonous scheme instigated by the British and other foreigners. Yet Brazilians did form their own abolition movement. Joaquim Nabuco, an elite parliamentary leader who had previously been exiled in London, formed the Brazilian

---

[2]Compiled from information in Leslie Bethell (ed.), *Brazil: Empire and Republic, 1822–1930* (Cambridge: Cambridge University Press, 1989).

Anti-Slavery Society in 1880. Many of the Society's supporters were free people of color, including boatmen and railway workers who refused to transport slaves. Abolitionists persuaded some small slave-holders to free their slaves, and they assisted the increasing numbers of slaves who fled their masters.

A massive exodus of slaves, like something out of the Hebrew Bible, finally killed slavery in Brazil. First, in 1883–84, in the far northeast, members of various social classes united to prevent slaves from being sold and transported south. Slaves were freed one by one as citizens raised funds to compensate the slaves' owners. This sudden liberation, and similar events elsewhere in northern Brazil, inspired abolitionists throughout the country and helped legislators in 1886 outlaw whipping as punishment for slaves. Then, in spite of planters' determination to resist all antislavery measures, slaves began fleeing the great coffee plantations around São Paulo begin-ning in 1887. Thousands deserted their masters. Although the fugitives had no invading army to protect them, as in the American Civil War, a large secret network of abolitionists provided shelter in trains and in shantytowns and in some cases even found jobs for the runaways. Brazilian police and armed forces refused or were unable to pursue them.

Political and economic elites scrambled to retake the initiative. São Paulo's planters, frantically trying to salvage their crops, began to free large numbers of slaves in return for service contracts that would keep them in the fields. The provincial government, following on their heels, freed all slaves through legislative action, while also subsidizing the immigration of another 90,000 Europeans to work on the coffee estates. Their arrival in 1888 crucially helped to resolve the planters' labor crisis.

While the emperor Dom Pedro II was away in Europe, his daughter, Princess Isabel, acted as Regent. On May 13, 1888, respond-ing to the collapse of slavery as a workable system and yielding to pressures from the abolitionists, she signed the so-called "Golden Law" (*Lei Áurea*), abolishing slavery in Brazil immediately and without compensation to slaveholders. Angry planters withdrew their support of the monarchy, which collapsed in a military coup the following year.

Like most of those in the Americas, former slaves in Brazil were freed from the evils of human bondage but sank to the lowest levels of a stratified society. After abolition, reformers never seriously considered land redistribution and failed to provide any educational measures for former slaves. In the sugar-producing northeast, Afro-Brazilians remained as wage laborers and tenants on the plantations. In the coffee region of the southeast, however, planters and their government allies flooded the labor market with subsidized European immigrants who were willing to work at wages and under conditions unacceptable to ex-slaves. Some Afro-Brazilians migrated to the rapidly developing cities of São Paulo and Rio de Janeiro. There, however, European immigrants monopolized the best jobs, and Afro-Brazilians were left with menial, low-wage employment. While former slaves and their descendants struggled for their livelihoods and dignity, elites interpreted their continuing poverty as proof of innate racial inferiority.

RACISM IN THE AMERICAS

The end of the slave trade and slavery did not remove its ideological legacy: white supremacy. Whether or not the slave trade and slavery *caused* Europeans and Euro-Americans to believe that people of African descent were inherently inferior to themselves (as discussed in Chapter 1), racism quickly became a fundamental feature of the exploitation inherent in slavery. Racial regimes took shape differently in different places, from the sharp distinction between black and white in the United States to the multiple racial categories in Brazil, for example. But in every American society touched by slavery, the highest echelons were occupied by people categorized as "white" and the lowest were reserved for those with the darkest skin. "White" came to stand for civilization, intelligence, and virtue; "black" people were allegedly barbaric, crude, and prone to vice.

This way of looking at things helped slave societies function. The supposed inferiority of black to white justified the persistence of slavery and highlighted the dangers of freeing people allegedly unprepared for freedom. Moreover, white supremacy infected non-slaveholding whites, cementing their support for slavery and defining the limits of dissent, and black people too, whose souls and self-esteem were beaten even more than their bodies. Exploitation and violence were rationalized with the assertion that the victims were unfit for anything else. It was something about the *slave*, slaveholders and their allies came to believe, that justified slavery.

This type of thinking did not just disappear with the abolition of slavery, but as a social and historical phenomenon, racism did change over time. By the mid- to late 19th century, as New World slavery was coming to an end, European and Euro-American frustration with postemancipation societies coincided with a new kind of racial thinking: "scientific" (or really pseudo-scientific) racism. Emerging from the Enlightenment impetus to classify and rank natural phenomena, "scientific" racism held that their differing physical features distinguished Europeans, Africans, Asians, and aboriginal Americans as members of biologically distinct "races." Scientifically measurable physical differences were also expressed, racial thinkers believed, in cultural differences; so culture was a result of biology and therefore only partially changeable. The differing qualities and abilities of the various "races" allowed them to be ranked; and not surprisingly, considering who was behind these views, Europeans were believed to be the superior race.

"Scientific" racism justified the continued disfranchisement and exploitation of ex-slaves throughout the Americas. Black people, as distinct from and inferior to whites, the thinking went, were not fit for citizenship. In Western Europe and the United States, this new racism also laid the ideological foundations for imperialism. Dark-skinned peoples in Africa and parts of Asia were defined as irredeemably savage, uncivilized primitives, with enormous sex drives but with little desire for work or material gain. Those with political ambitions, economic designs, or missionary impulses generally agreed: since "the natives" had no inner controls, it became the "white man's burden" to dominate and discipline them.

Yesterday's science is today's commonsense and tomorrow's nonsense. The "scientific" racism of the 19th century—with its associated head measuring, elaboration of racial "types," and sometimes deadly eugenic impulses—formed the basis of commonplace assumptions about race in the modern Western world. We now know with certainty that "race" really is skin deep: in 1997 the Human Genome Diversity Project took blood samples from members of over 400 different ethnic groups and concluded that 99.99 percent of all people's genetic makeup is the same. Furthermore, the tiny remaining genetic variations do not break down along "racial" lines. Yet although biological "race" is a fiction, it still is a meaningful category with a powerful history. Tragically, we live with its persistent material and ideological ramifications to this day.

SLAVERY IN THE CONTEMPORARY WORLD

In December 2006, UN Secretary General Kofi Annan marked the International Day for the Abolition of Slavery with a public statement linking the past and the present. "On 25 March 2007," he wrote, "the world will mark the two hundredth anniversary of the abolition of the slave trade in the British colonies. This landmark will be a powerful reminder of centuries of struggle and progress in combating slavery—but also of the fact that we still have not managed to eliminate it completely." He referred to the continuing existence of slavery in some parts of the world, as well as new forms of unfree labor and human trafficking.

In spite of worldwide ideological opposition to chattel slavery, it is still widespread in such Saharan nations as Niger, Mauritania, Chad, and Sudan, affecting an estimated 20 million people. Such "traditional" bondage is immensely overshadowed by what modern antislavery groups describe as "new forms" of slavery, however: men, women, and children are physically forced to work, often under meaningless contracts, in a range of occupations in industrial as well as less-developed countries. Such modern slaves include Indian boys herding camels in Arabia, porters and domestic servants in Africa, carpet factory workers in India, sweatshop workers in Thailand, and countless others. Contract laborers, migrant workers, and refugees are enticed or sold into work from which they cannot escape without repaying the cost of their transport, and sometimes charges for shelter, food, and even the tools with which they work as well. Debtors become exploited, forced laborers for their creditors, who include moneylenders in East Asia, landlords in Latin America, subcontractors clearing the forest in Brazil, factory owners in India, labor recruiters in Philippines, pimps in Europe, Japan, or the United States, and more. Poverty-stricken parents also sell their children, or are misled into turning them over, into forced labor, in which many suffer from overwork and malnutrition. Altogether some 27 million people suffer in slavery today—slightly less than the entire population of Canada—including an estimated 30,000 to 40,000 people in the United States.

Contemporary forced labor—whether debt bondage, contract labor, child labor, or forced prostitution—is sustained by a lively slave trade, or "human trafficking" as it is now called. Untold thousands of "sex slaves"—often girls or young women who have volunteered for decent-sounding jobs, only to find themselves coerced into prostitution—are trafficked across borders, particularly in Eastern Europe and South Asia. Children are also bought and sold within and across national borders, forced into domestic service, work in markets, or as cheap farm labor. UNICEF estimates that more than 200,000 children are trafficked in West and Central Africa each year. Precise numbers are impossible to obtain, but according to the U.S. Central Intelligence Agency, between 700,000 and 2 million people are trafficked across all borders each year, including more than 50,000 people a year brought to the United States. Human trafficking has become the third largest money earner for organized crime, after drugs and guns.

THE BIG LESSONS

It may be tempting to see the material presented in this book, and even in this Epilogue, as confirmation of life's brutality, violence, and degradation. Abolition led not so much to the end of white supremacy and the beginnings of more equitable relationships between Africans and Europeans, but to new kinds of racism and new forms of exploitation. Although the Atlantic slave trade between Africa and the Americas has ended, human trafficking has not. But are there other, less pessimistic, lessons as well?

For hundreds if not thousands of years, people all over the world believed that slavery was an unchanging piece of the social fabric. No one wanted to be a slave himself or herself, and there have been revolts against slavery since at least the time of Spartacus, but it seemed unthinkable that the institution could be abolished, or at least universally condemned. But as the anthropologist Margaret Mead said, one should never doubt that a small group of thoughtful, committed citizens can change the world—indeed, it is the only thing that ever has. If you think that our world has to be the way it is, with all of its inequities, injustices, and violence, then what have you learned from Toussaint L'Ouverture, Dona Beatrix Kimpa Vita, or the thousands of slaves who freed themselves in the upheavals of the 19th century? Granville Sharp, Olaudah Equiano, and the millions of petitioners and sugar boycotters who helped to end the Atlantic slave trade should teach us the value of individual as well as collective activism. And those many thousands gone—the captured and the coffled, those tossed about in the noxious bellies of slave ships, the auctioned and whipped, the raped and tortured—they built this world that we live in. From the slave ship, as historian Ali Mazrui has put it, they brought us the space ship.

But monumental as the economic contributions of the enslaved were to Western development, people of African descent have given us more than that. The music of African-descended people, to take one example, is the most popular and imitated all over the world. And there is more: in literature and art, style and slang, politics and poetry, from hip hop to slam dunk, people in all corners of the globe imbibe the culture of the descendants of Africa. Why? Perhaps because in the face of terrible struggle, African, African American, Afro-Brazilian, Afro-Caribbean, and Afro-European culture offers a vision of freedom and humanity. It takes tragedy and offers hope, creativity, and vitality. It shouts from the rooftops, "I am not an object, to be bought and sold; I am human, with all of the talents, frailties, dreams and fears of the human race."

History does not just happen, unfolding naturally like the seasons or rising and falling like tides. People make history, bending and shaping the present to create the future. The history of the Atlantic slave trade teaches us that the coerced, backbreaking efforts of Africans and their descendants vitally shaped the world we inhabit, even if they have not shared fairly in the fruits of their labor. It also teaches us that white supremacy was not inevitable, but rather was built over 400 years by human agency. It took shape differently at different times and places, as the contrasting examples of postemancipation Jamaica, Cuba, Brazil, and the United States show. Its legacies persist, in the Americas as well as in the troubled continent of Africa. A well-known Nigerian slogan says that "no condition is permanent." Perhaps, as we credit two centuries of antislavery activism with changing the modern world, that is a lesson to remember too.

liography

GENERAL WORKS ON THE SLAVE TRADE

Until the second edition of the Transatlantic Slave Trade Database is available (expected to be published on the World Wide Web in 2008), the place to start for an overview of the volume and contours of the transatlantic slave trade is David Eltis' article, "The Volume and Structure of the Transatlantic Slave Trade: A Reassessment," *William and Mary Quarterly*, 3rd Series, 58, 1 (2001): 17–46, which draws on data from the invaluable resource, *The Trans-Atlantic Slave Trade: A Database on CD-ROM*, edited by David Eltis, Stephen D. Behrendt, David Richardson, and Herbert S. Klein (1999). This research builds on the pioneering work of Philip Curtin in *The Atlantic Slave Trade: A Census* (1969). A preliminary summary of the forthcoming, revised version of the database is in David Eltis and David Richardson (eds.), "Introduction," in *Extending the Frontiers: Essays on the New Transatlantic Slave Trade Database* (Yale University Press, forthcoming).

More narrative overviews include the Mariners' Museum's beautifully illustrated *Captive Passage: The Transatlantic Slave Trade and the Making of the Americas* (2002); Herbert S. Klein, *The Atlantic Slave Trade* (1999); Basil Davidson, *The African Slave Trade* (rev. and expanded ed., 1980); Joseph E. Inikori (ed.), *Forced Migration: The Impact of the Export Slave Trade on African Societies* (1982); and Joseph E. Inikori and Stanley L. Engerman (eds.), *The Atlantic Slave Trade: Effects on Economies, Societies, and Peoples in Africa, the Americas, and Europe* (1992). John Thornton's *Africa and Africans in the Making of the Atlantic World, 1400–1800* (2nd ed. 1998) and David Eltis' *The Rise of African Slavery in the Americas* (2000) both offer large-scale views of the slave trade, but with differing emphases and interpretations. David Northrup (ed.), *The Atlantic Slave Trade* (2nd ed. 2002) is a reader containing excerpts of important primary and secondary sources on the Atlantic slave trade, while Elizabeth Donnan (ed.), *Documents Illustrative of the History of the Slave Trade to America*, 4 vols. (1930–35) remains the most comprehensive published collection of primary sources.

For a visual sense of the slave trade's routes, along with helpful introductions, see James Walvin's *Atlas of Slavery* (2006). *The Atlantic Slave Trade and Slave Life in the Americas: A Visual Record*, compiled by Jerome S. Handler and Michael L. Tuite, Jr. at the University of Virginia, is an extensive online collection of images, a few of which are in this book. It is available at http://hitchcock.itc.virginia.edu/Slavery/index.php.

The most descriptive and moving renditions of the slave trade include an unconventional history book and a novel. In *The Diligent: A Voyage through the Worlds of the Slave Trade* (2002), historian Robert Harms uses one ship's voyage to illuminate dynamics in France, West Africa, the Caribbean, and at sea, telling fascinating stories (including that of Bulfinche Lambe) in the process. Barry Unsworth's novel *Sacred Hunger* (1992) is simply the most magnificent depiction of the slave trade one can read. It will rattle your bones.

THE SLAVE TRADE AND THE AMERICAS

An extensive body of writing now deals with slavery in the Americas, as *Slavery and Slaving in World History: A Bibliography*, edited by Joseph C. Miller (1999), and the annual bibliographies in the journal *Slavery and Abolition* show. Three encyclopedias—the *Macmillan Encyclopedia of World Slavery*, edited by Paul Finkelman and Joseph C. Miller (1998); *A Historical Guide to World Slavery*, edited by Seymour Drescher and Stanley L. Engerman (1998); and *The Historical Encyclopedia of World Slavery*, with Junius P. Rodriguez, general editor (1997)—also provide information on every topic imaginable with reference to slavery.

Some of the most useful overviews dealing with the slave trade and the development of New World slavery are Philip D. Curtin, *The Rise and Fall of the Plantation Complex: Essays in Atlantic History* (2nd ed. 1998); Robin Blackburn, *The Making of New World Slavery* (1997); and David Brion Davis, *Inhuman Bondage: The Rise and Fall of Slavery in the New World* (2006) and his earlier *Slavery and Human Progress* (1984). On trade and cultural links specifically between West Africa and Brazil, see Pierre Verger, *Trade Relations between the Bight of Benin and Bahia from the 17th to 19th Century* (1976). For the United States, Ira Berlin's *Many Thousands Gone: The First Two Centuries of Slavery in North America* (1988) and *Generations of Captivity: A History of African-American Slaves* (2003) are both magisterial overviews. Both include the story of Anthony Johnson, as does the extremely useful website *Africans in America*, at http://www.pbs.org/wgbh/aia/home.html. The companion to a PBS series, it includes overview narratives, images, biographies, maps, and resources for teachers. Haile Gerima's moving and graphic film *Sankofa* (1994, 125 minutes) dramatizes the slave trade and slavery in the Americas through the life of one woman.

Some of the most important monographs on slavery and race in the United States, particularly during its colonial period, include Winthrop D. Jordan, *White over Black: American Attitudes toward the Negro, 1550–1812* (1968); Peter Wood, *Black Majority: Negroes in Colonial South Carolina from 1670 through the Stono Rebellion* (1974); and Phillip D. Morgan, *Slave Counterpoint: Black Culture in the Eighteenth-Century Chesapeake and Lowcountry* (1998).

THE SLAVE TRADE AND AFRICA

These days, the most important single book on the African dynamics of the Atlantic slave trade is John Thornton's *Africa and Africans in the Making of the Atlantic World*, mentioned above. Paul E. Lovejoy's *Transformations in Slavery: A History of Slavery in Africa* (1983) and Patrick Manning's *Slavery and African Life: Occidental, Oriental, and African Slave Trades* (1990) are also impressive broad treatments of the slave trade in Africa. In *How Europe Underdeveloped Africa* (1972), Walter Rodney addresses the effects of the slave trade on African (under)development. Patrick Manning's demographic simulation of the effects of the slave trade on Africa's population, in which users can change variables themselves to explore possible scenarios, is available online at http://www.worldhistorynetwork.org/migrationsim/index.html.

Joseph C. Miller's monumental and brilliant *Way of Death: Merchant Capitalism and the Angolan Slave Trade* (1988) illuminates the structures, processes, and horrors of the Central African trade between Portugal, Angola, and Brazil. Other examinations of specific African regions include Walter Rodney, *A History of the Upper Guinea Coast, 1545–1800* (1970); Boubacar Barry, *Senegambia and the Atlantic Slave Trade* (1998); Richard Roberts, *Warriors, Merchants, and Slaves: The State and the Economy in the Middle Niger Valley, 1700–1914* (1987); Sandra Greene, *Gender, Ethnicity, and Social Change on the Upper Slave Coast: A History of the Anlo-Ewe* (1996); Patrick Manning, *Slavery, Colonialism and Economic Growth in Dahomey, 1640–1960* (1982); and Walter Hawthorne, *Planting Rice and Harvesting Slaves: Transformations along the Guinea-Bissau Coast, 1400–1900* (2003). William St. Clair's *The Grand Slave Emporium: Cape Coast Castle and the British Slave Trade* (2006) depicts slave traders, the enslaved, and Africans who worked at this one trading station, in the context of larger Atlantic trends.

While many of those sources refer to African resistance against the slave trade, this is the major theme of Sylviane A. Diouf (ed.), *Fighting the Slave Trade: West African Strategies* (2003). John Thornton's book, *The Kongolese Saint Anthony: Donna Beatriz Kimpa Vita and the Antonian Movement, 1684–1706* (1999), tells the story recounted in Chapter 2, emphasizing the Antonian movement as a revolt against slave trade–driven warfare. The dramatic film *Andanggaman*, directed by Roger Gnoan M'Bala (2002, 90 minutes), focuses on slaving in West Africa and depicts a young man's struggle to rescue his captive mother.

THE MIDDLE PASSAGE AND ENSLAVED PEOPLE'S EXPERIENCES

In addition to the firsthand accounts listed below and the general overviews listed above, information on the Middle Passage is available in Herbert S. Klein, *The Middle Passage: Comparative Studies in the Atlantic Slave Trade* (1978) and Michael Gomez, *Exchanging our Country Marks: The Transformation of African Identities in the Colonial and Antebellum South* (1998). Joseph Miller's *Way of Death* (listed earlier) details the conditions and mortality during slaves' passages from the interior to the coast, in the Middle Passage, and into Brazilian slavery. In *Saltwater Slavery: A Middle Passage from Africa to the American Diaspora* (2007), Stephanie E. Smallwood examines the trade between the Gold Coast and British North America between 1675 and 1725, sensitively and imaginatively attending to the physical and psychological experiences of the trade's victims at every stage of their forced migrations. David Richardson's article, "Shipboard Revolts, African Authority, and the Atlantic Slave Trade," *William and Mary Quarterly* 58, 1 (2001): 69–91 makes the case that resistance was not futile, a point more fully developed in Eric Robert Taylor's book, *If We Must Die: Shipboard Insurrections in the Era of the Atlantic Slave Trade* (2006). The best film depiction of the Middle Passage is in Steven Spielberg's film *Amistad* (1997, 155 minutes).

The most influential proponents of relatively rapid creolization among slaves in the Americas have been two anthropologists, Sidney Mintz and Richard Price, especially in their book *The Birth of African-American Culture: An Anthropological Perspective* (1992). Phillip Morgan, in "The Cultural Implications of the Atlantic Slave Trade: African Regional Origins, American Destinations and New World Developments," *Slavery and Abolition* 18 (1997): 122–45, also suggests early and significant cultural mixing within enslaved populations. On the other side, arguing that Africans maintained their own distinct cultural elements for longer than has been previously thought, are Paul Lovejoy, in (among other publications) "The African Diaspora: Revisionist Interpretations of Ethnicity, Culture and Religion under Slavery," *Studies in the World History of Slavery, Abolition, and Emancipation* II, 1 (1997) at http://www.h-et.msu.edu/-slavery/essays/esy9701 love.html and John Thornton in *Africa and Africans* (referenced earlier). Other fascinating studies of slaves *as Africans* in the New World include Michael Gomez, *Exchanging our Country Marks* (listed already); Gwendolyn Midlo Hall, *Africans in Colonial Louisiana: The Development of Afro-Creole Culture in the Eighteenth Century* (1992) and *Slavery and African Ethnicities in the Americas: Restoring the Links* (2005); James Sweet, *Recreating Africa: Culture, Kinship, and Religion in the African-Portuguese World, 1441–1770* (2003); Linda M. Heywood (ed.), *Central Africans and Cultural Transformations in the American Diaspora* (2002); John Thornton, "The African Experience of the '20 and Odd Negroes' Arriving in Virginia in 1619," *William and Mary Quarterly*, 3rd Series, 55, 3 (1998): 421–34; John K. Thornton, "African Dimensions of the Stono Rebellion," *American Historical Review* 96, 4 (1991): 1101–13; Franklin W. Knight, *The African Dimension in Latin American Societies* (1974); Margaret Washington Creel, *"A Peculiar People": Slave Religion and Community Culture among the Gullahs* (1988); Michael Mullin, *Africa in America: Slave Acculturation and Resistance in the American South and the British Caribbean, 1736–1831* (1992); and the film *Sankofa* (mentioned above). *The Language You Cry In: The Story of a Mende Song*, directed by Alvaro Toepke and Angel Serrano (1998, 52 minutes), is a moving documentary film which connects coastal Georgia and Sierra Leone through women in each place who know the same funeral song.

A useful sampling of the literature on maroons begins with Richard Price, *Maroon Societies: Rebel Slave Communities in the Americas* (1979) and the chapter on runaways in Thornton's *Africa and Africans*. See also, for Brazil, Stuart B. Schwartz, "Rethinking Palmares: Slave Resistance in Colonial Brazil," in *Slaves, Peasants, and Rebels: Reconsidering Brazilian Slavery* (1992) and, for Jamaica, Kenneth M. Bilby, *True-Born Maroons* (2005). The highly stylized film *Quilombo*, by Carlos Diegues (1984, 114 minutes), dramatizes the culture and final downfall of Palmares.

SOME FIRSTHAND ACCOUNTS OF THE SLAVE TRADE

Nearly all of the narratives by former participants of the slave trade (slavers or, less often, the enslaved) were written by men, and were written as part of the abolitionist movement. The most famous is *The Interesting Narrative of Olaudah Equiano, or Gustavus Vassa, the African* (1793). A useful modern edition is *The Interesting Narrative of the Life of Olaudah Equiano Written by Himself, with Related Documents*, edited with an introduction by Robert J. Allison, published in the Bedford Series in History and Culture (2nd ed. 2007). Vincent Carretta's biography, *Equiano, the African: Biography of a Self-Made Man* (2005), argues that Equiano was born in South Carolina and not, as is written in the autobiography, present-day Nigeria. Among those who still believe Equiano's account of his origins is Paul E. Lovejoy, in "Autobiography and Memory: Gustavus Vassa, alias Olaudah Equiano, the African," *Slavery and Abolition* 27, 3 (2006): 317–47.

Philip D. Curtin (ed.). *Africa Remembered: Narratives by West Africans from the Era of the Slave Trade* (1967) contains chapter-length accounts with introductions by scholars.

Book-length narratives by the formerly enslaved include James Albert Ukawsaw Gronniosaw, *A Narrative of the Most Remarkable Particulars in the Life of James Albert Ukawsaw Gronniosaw, an African Prince* (1770); Venture Smith, *A Narrative of the Life and Adventures of Venture, a Native of Africa: But Resident above Sixty Years in the United States of America. Related by Himself* (1798); Boyrereau Brinch, *The Blind African Slave, or Memoirs of Boyrereau Brinch, Nick-Named Jeffrey Brace* (1810); Thomas Bluett, *Some Memoirs of the Life of Job, the Son of Solomon* (1734); and Ottobah Cugoano, *Thoughts and Sentiments on the Evil of Slavery* (1787). Robin Law and Paul E. Lovejoy (eds.), *The Biography of Mahommah Gardo Baquaqua: His Passage from Slavery to Freedom in Africa and America* (2001) is the only published narrative from a survivor of the Middle Passage to Brazil.

Personal accounts of the trade by slavers and ex-slavers include Theophilus Conneau, *A Slaver's Log Book: Or 20 Years' Residence in Africa, The Original Manuscript* (1976); Bruce L. Mouser (ed.), *A Slaving Voyage to Africa and Jamaica: The Log of the Sandown, 1793–1794* (2002); Jean Barbot, "A Description of the Coasts of North and South Guinea" (1732), in Thomas Astley and John Churchill (eds.), *Collection of Voyages and Travels;* Alexander Falconbridge, *An Account of the Slave Trade on the Coast of Africa* (1788); Isidore Paiewonsky, *Eyewitness Accounts of Slavery in the Danish West Indies: Also Graphic Tales of Other Slave Happenings on Ships and Plantations* (1989); Robert Norris, *Memoirs of the Reign of Bossa Ahádee, King of Dahomy, an Inland Country of Guiney, to which are added the author's journey to Abomey, the capital, and a short account of the African slave trade* (1968); P.E.H. Hair, Adam Jones, and Robin Law (eds.), *Barbot on Guinea: The Writings of Jean Barbot on West Africa 1678–1712* (1992); John Newton, *Thoughts upon the African Slave Trade* (1788); William Snelgrave, *A New Account of Some Parts of Guinea and the Slave-Trade* (1734); and John Atkins, *A Voyage to Guinea, Brazil, and the West-Indies; in His Majesty's Ships, the Swallow and Weymouth* (1735).

The only slave trade-related memoir written by a woman is Anna Maria Falconbridge, *Narrative of Two Voyages to the River Sierra Leone During the Years 1791–1792–1793* (2000). Anna Falconbridge was the wife of Alexander Falconbridge, and her disgruntled narrative covers the period when he was British governor of Sierra Leone.

ABOLITION OF THE SLAVE TRADE

In spite of six decades of scrutiny, the major work on slavery's impact on Britain remains Eric Williams, *Capitalism and Slavery* (1944). One of the more important reassessments, which accords with Williams on key points, is J.E. Inikori, *Africans and the Industrial Revolution in England: A Study in International Trade and Economic Development* (2002). For a refutation of the thesis that the slave trade and slavery were abolished because they were unprofitable, see Seymour Drescher, *Econocide: British Slavery in the Era of Abolition* (1977) and David Eltis, *Economic Growth and the Ending of the Transatlantic Slave Trade* (1987). The following books also deal broadly with the British antislavery movement: Suzanne Miers, *Britain and the Ending of the Slave Trade* (1974); David Brion Davis, *The Problem of Slavery in the Age of Revolution, 1770–1823* (1975); Robin Blackburn, *The Overthrow of Colonial Slavery, 1776–1848* (1988); and the highly readable narrative account by Adam Hochschild, *Bury the Chains: Prophets and Rebels in the Fight to Free an Empire's Slaves* (2005). The dramatic film *Amazing Grace,* directed by Michael Apted (2007, 111 minutes), depicts the British movement to end the slave trade, while Steven Spielberg's *Amistad* (listed earlier) centers on a U.S. Supreme Court case dealing with the illegal slave trade in the 1830s.

On the American Revolution and the slave trade, see Simon Schama, *Rough Crossings: Britain, the Slaves and the American Revolution* (2005) and Cassandra Pybus, *Epic Journeys of Freedom: Runaway Slaves of the American Revolution and their Global Quest for Liberty* (2006). For the Haitian Revolution, the early, seminal work was

C.L.R. James, *The Black Jacobins: Toussaint L'Ouverture and the San Domingo Revolution* (1938). Important reassessments, which include more attention to the African role in Haiti and the revolution's importance in an Atlantic context, include Carolyn E. Fick, *The Making of Haiti: The Saint Domingue Revolution from Below* (1990); David Patrick Geggus, *The Impact of the Haitian Revolution in the Atlantic World* (2001); Laurent Dubois, *Avengers of the New World: The Story of the Haitian Revolution* (2004); and John Thornton, " 'I am the Subject of the King of Congo': African Political Ideology and the Haitian Revolution," *Journal of World History* 4, 2 (1993): 181–213.

On the transition away from slaving in Africa, see Robin Law (ed.), *From Slave Trade to "Legitimate" Commerce: The Commercial Transition in Nineteenth-Century West Africa* (1995). On the founding of the Sierra Leone colony, one could use John Peterson, *Province of Freedom; A History of Sierra Leone, 1787–1870* (1969), while Jean Herskovits Kopytoff's book, *A Preface to Modern Nigeria: The "Sierra Leonians" in Yoruba, 1830–1890* (1965) deals with the "recaptives" and their descendants who fanned out from Sierra Leone.

AFTER THE TRANSATLANTIC SLAVE TRADE

Many of the works listed above are also relevant for understanding slave emancipation itself. For the importance of West Indian slave revolts in British Empire emancipation, see also Michael Craton, *Testing the Chains: Resistance to Slavery in the British West Indies* (1982). David Brion Davis' *Inhuman Bondage* (listed already) contains extensive information about emancipation throughout the Americas, including several chapters on the United States. There is, of course, an enormous body of historical writing on the American Civil War, which will not be surveyed here. For emancipation in Brazil and Cuba, excellent places to start reading are Robert Edgar Conrad, *The Destruction of Brazilian Slavery, 1850–1888* (1993 [orig. 1972]) and Rebecca J. Scott, *Slave Emancipation in Cuba: The Transition to Free Labor, 1860–1899* (1985). *Gender and Slave Emancipation in the Atlantic World,* edited by Pamela Scully and Diana Paton (2005) is one of the few studies to treat gender, slavery, and freedom together.

The resources for studying freed people in postemancipation societies are voluminous, but a convenient entrée into the primary and secondary sources is through Rebecca J. Scott et al. (eds.), *Societies after Slavery: A Select Annotated Bibliography of Printed Sources on Cuba, Brazil, British Colonial Africa, South Africa, and the British West Indies* (2002). There are also several very useful comparative overviews: Frederick Cooper, Thomas C. Holt, and Rebecca J. Scott, *Beyond Slavery: Explorations of Race, Labor, and Citizenship in Postemancipation Societies* (2000); Rebecca J. Scott, "Defining the Boundaries of Freedom in the World of Cane: Cuba, Brazil, and Louisiana after Emancipation," *American Historical Review* 99, 1 (1994): 70–103; and Rebecca J. Scott, "Exploring the Meaning of Freedom: Postemancipation Societies in Comparative Perspective," *The Hispanic American Historical Review* 68, 3 (1988): 407–28. Also see Thomas C. Holt's wide-ranging and important book, *The Problem of Freedom: Race, Labor, and Politics in Jamaica and Britain, 1832–1938* (1992), which deals not only with developments in Jamaica, but with the evolving Western thinking on race.

Frederick Cooper's chapter in *Beyond Slavery* (listed above) treats the relationship between antislavery and European imperialism in Africa. On this topic, also see Patrick Brantlinger's illuminating essay, "Victorians and Africans: The Genealogy of the Myth of the Dark Continent," in Henry Louis Gates, Jr. (ed.), *"Race," Writing and Difference* (1986). Similarly, see Seymour Drescher, "The Ending of the Slave Trade and the Evolution of European Scientific Racism," *Social Science History* 14, 3 (1990): 415–50.

On modern-day slave trading, the most comprehensive source is Kevin Bales, *Disposable People: New Slavery in the Global Economy* (2004). The resources at Antislavery International's website, http://www.antislavery.org, are up-to-date and instructive.

Index